# THE RAMAYANA CODE

## Ancient Wisdom for Modern Success

## PRAVEEN SHARMA

INDIA • SINGAPORE • MALAYSIA

ISBN  979-8-89277-827-5

# Contents

# Acknowledgement

In crafting "The Ramayana Code," a journey illuminated by the timeless wisdom of the Ramayana, the unwavering support and insights from those closest to me have been my guiding stars. To my mother, Kamlesh Sharma, whose encouragement to delve deeply into Hindu mythology sparked the inception of this book, I owe a world of gratitude. My wife, Nisha Sharma, has been instrumental in shaping the content, turning abstract ideas into tangible wisdom. My daughter, Ashrika, at the tender age of eight, asked profound "Why" questions, igniting critical thinking that enriched this manuscript. Naveen Sharma, my brother, planted the seed of inspiration to share my interpretations of the Ramayana. Pushp Sharma, my sister, meticulously proofread the drafts, ensuring clarity and coherence. Abhinav, my brother-in-law, with his keen insight and unwavering support, has been a silent pillar of strength. His ability to offer perspective during critical moments of doubt and his enthusiasm for the project's vision have been invaluable in navigating the complex journey of bringing this book to fruition. Anuj and Chanchal Sharma, through their embodiment of relationship ideals, provided a living example that fueled my writing. My friends — Rahul, Deshant, Isha, and Daizy — patiently listened and provided feedback that was crucial in refining the book's flow.

To my mother, your stories and faith have been the foundation of my journey; your wisdom threads through every page. To my daughter, Ashrika, your curiosity and innocence remind us that wisdom often comes from the simplest questions.

This book is a testament to the collective spirit and dedication of all who contributed, each playing a unique role in bringing "The Ramayana Code" to life.

# Chapter 1

# Lantern of Wisdom: Reflecting on Ramayan's Eternal Guidance

My earliest memories of the Ramayana stem from the enchanting evenings spent under the starlit sky, where my grandmother, a master storyteller, would weave tales from this grand epic. Her stories were a vibrant kaleidoscope of heroic ballads and moral fables, each narrated with such fervor and detail that the characters seemed to come alive in the dim glow of our lantern. These were not mere bedtime tales; they were profound narratives of valor, sacrifice, and wisdom. With every story of Rama's unwavering duty, Sita's profound strength, and Hanuman's unparalleled devotion, she painted a picture of a world where righteousness and moral fortitude reigned supreme. As I journeyed from childhood to adulthood, these stories evolved in their meaning for me. The Ramayana transformed from a collection of mythical adventures into a reservoir of guidance, reflecting back my own life's struggles and triumphs, becoming a beacon during times of moral ambiguity and ethical dilemmas.

> Fun Fact
>
> Before composing the Ramayana, Valmiki was a bandit named Ratnakara. His transformation into a sage and poet is a testament to personal growth and redemption, mirroring the profound changes characters undergo in the epic.

## Unveiling the Epic: More Than Just a Tale

Attributed to the sage Valmiki, the Ramayana is a rich mosaic of adventure, romance, and philosophy. Spanning 24,000 verses, it chronicles the life of Prince Rama, his steadfast commitment to dharma (duty), the abduction of his wife Sita, and the ensuing battle with the demon king Ravana. However, to merely recount its plot is to miss its true significance – the Ramayana is more than a story; it's a comprehensive guide for understanding the intricacies of human life and morality.

## The Timeless Appeal of the Ramayana

This epic's universality lies in its ability to transcend time and culture, resonating with essential human experiences and emotions. Its exploration of dharma, relationships, and the eternal struggle between good and evil, offers insights as relevant today as they were millennia ago.

## Ancient Wisdom for Modern Times

The teachings of the Ramayana remain profoundly relevant in the contemporary world, offering timeless wisdom applicable to various aspects of modern life:

1. **Ethics and Integrity:** The epic serves as a moral compass, guiding us through the complex maze of ethical dilemmas

and integrity challenges prevalent in today's society. It encourages us to uphold virtue, even in the face of adversity.

2. **Leadership Principles:**   The ideal of 'Ram Rajya' stands as a model for exemplary governance, emphasizing welfare, justice, and the overall happiness of the community. These principles are foundational for effective and compassionate leadership in the modern era.

3. **Resilience and Perseverance:**   The trials and triumphs of the characters exemplify resilience, a vital attribute in our fast-paced and often unpredictable lives. Their journeys inspire us to persevere through challenges with grace and determination.

4. **Relationship Dynamics:**   The Ramayana illuminates the intricacies of various relationships, providing insights into nurturing and sustaining these bonds within our contemporary social fabric. It explores the nuances of familial, romantic, and platonic relationships with depth and empathy.

5. **Inner Transformation:** The climactic battle against Ravana transcends the physical realm, symbolizing the eternal struggle against our inner demons or negative impulses. This allegory inspires us to introspect and conquer our personal shortcomings, leading to profound self-improvement and inner growth.

## A Glimpse into the Journey Ahead

In the chapters to come, we will delve into these themes deeply. We will explore how Rama's adherence to dharma can guide our career choices, how Sita's resilience can inspire us in personal crises, and how Hanuman's devotion is relevant in building lasting relationships. Each chapter will unwrap these ancient tales to reveal kernels of wisdom applicable in our modern lives.

## Embracing the Timeless Wisdom

As we embark on this journey together, let us ponder – how can millennia-old stories illuminate our path today? The Ramayana is not a distant echo of the past; it is a living, breathing guide, as relevant now as it was when first composed. It invites us to look inward, to challenge ourselves, and to aspire to a life of purpose and fulfillment. The lessons it holds are not merely tales of an era gone by; they are beacons for our journey ahead, guiding us through the complexities of modern existence. In embracing the Ramayana's teachings, we might ask ourselves, "Is the Ramayana not only a timeless guide but also a mirror reflecting our own evolution?" This question invites us to explore not just the epic's wisdom, but also our personal growth and transformation as we navigate through life's myriad paths.

## Some Facts About Ramayana That You Might Find Fascinating

1.  The Ramayana is considered the longest epic poem *ever written*, clocking in at over 24,000 verses? That's more than ten times the length of the Odyssey and roughly three times the length of the Mahabharata, another epic poem from India! (Keep in mind that the exact length of the Ramayana can vary depending on the version.)

2.  The Ramayana, with its 24,000 verses, holds a hidden message within. The first letter of each verse, when combined in sequence, forms the complete Gayatri Mantra, a sacred chant considered the essence of the Vedas.

3.  Most know of Rama's brothers, but few are aware of his elder sister, Shanta. Sent away as a baby to protect her from

a curse, she reappears later, playing a crucial role in the epic. During Rama's exile, he encounters Shanta and her husband Rishyasringa, a powerful sage. Rishyasringa provides Rama with a powerful army of monkeys, instrumental in his victory over Ravana.

4. Lakshmana, known for his unwavering loyalty, made a remarkable sacrifice. He invoked the goddess of sleep, Nidra, to stay awake and protect Rama and Sita during their exile. However, as a condition, someone else had to take his place, leading Urmila, his wife, to sleep for fourteen years.

5. Lakshmana's wife, Urmila, held a hidden identity in some versions, being an incarnation of Nidra, the goddess of sleep.

6. While Jatayu, the valiant vulture king, is known for his sacrifice defending Sita, lesser-known is his connection to Vishnu. Some versions mention him as a former king cursed to become a vulture, awaiting release through selfless service.

7. Each head of Ravana represented a different vice like Kama (Lust), Krodha (Anger), Lobha (Greed), Moh (Attachment), Mada (Pride), Maatsarya (Envy), Ahankaar (Ego), Chitta (Will), Manas (Mind), Bhuddhi (Intellect). When Rama severed his heads, he symbolically conquered these vices, showcasing the victory of good over evil on multiple levels.

8. There are over 300 known versions of the Ramayana across different cultures and languages. Each version has its unique adaptations, characters, and plots that reflect the local culture and traditions where it was told. This diversity highlights the Ramayana's universal themes and its ability to adapt to different cultural contexts.

9. Jambavan, the king of bears, is believed to be immortal and to have lived from the Satya Yuga (the era of truth) to the Dvapara Yuga (the era of the Mahabharata), playing crucial roles in both

the Ramayana and the Mahabharata. Jambavan is the one who reminds Hanuman of his immense powers, enabling him to leap across the ocean to Lanka.

10. According to some versions of the Ramayana and other texts, Hanuman had a son named Makardhwaja. Makardhwaja was born from a mighty fish that ingested a drop of Hanuman's sweat while he was bathing in the ocean. Makardhwaja later becomes the guard of Ahiravan, the ruler of the underworld, in some versions of the story.

# Chapter 2

# Dharma: Understanding Duty and Integrity

Visualize the defining moment in the Ramayana when Prince Rama, heir to the grand throne of Ayodhya, stands at the threshold of a monumental decision. This scene is steeped in the profound ethos of dharma – the principle of righteous duty that governs moral conduct. As Rama prepares to step into the forest, relinquishing the crown and comforts of palace life, he is not merely making a sacrifice; he is embodying the very essence of dharma.

The air is thick with a mix of admiration and sorrow as Rama, clad in the attire of an ascetic, bids farewell to his tearful subjects. This is not a journey into exile; it's a journey into the heart of duty, honor, and integrity. His decision reverberates through the kingdom, setting an example that transcends time. It's a moment that captures the agony of separation from his beloved wife, Sita, and his devoted brother, Lakshmana, who choose to join him, sharing in his commitment to uphold dharma.

In this pivotal moment, Rama's step into the forest symbolizes a step away from personal desire and towards a greater good. He walks the path of selflessness, illustrating that true leadership and nobility lie not in wielding power, but in the willingness to sacrifice for principle. The forest, with its uncertainties and challenges, becomes a metaphor for the trials and tribulations one faces when choosing duty over personal ambition.

As Rama disappears into the dense foliage, his footsteps echo a powerful message: that the path of dharma, though arduous and often fraught with sacrifice, is the path to true fulfillment and honor. This scene from the Ramayana is not just a narrative of a prince going into exile; it is a timeless lesson in prioritizing duty, responsibility, and ethical integrity over personal gain – a cornerstone of dharma that continues to resonate in the corridors of time.

Fun Fact

Some scholars interpret the Ramayana's detailed astronomical references to suggest the events could date back to around 5000 BCE, offering a fascinating blend of mythology and potential historical timelines.

## Diverse Manifestations of Dharma in the Ramayana

In the Ramayana, the multifaceted nature of dharma is not only embodied in the protagonist, Rama, but also illustrated through the actions and choices of a variety of characters, each offering a unique perspective on moral conduct.

Fun Fact

The Ramayana's influence extends globally, with adaptations like Indonesia's Wayang Kulit and Thailand's Ramakien, showcasing the epic's ability to resonate across diverse cultures and traditions.

At one end of this spectrum is Ravana, the formidable king of Lanka, whose life presents a powerful antithesis to Rama's adherence to dharma. Ravana, a character of immense strength and intellect, is ultimately undone by his own unchecked ambitions and desires. His abduction of Sita, driven by a blend of revenge and infatuation, marks a clear departure from the path of righteousness. This act, symbolizing the overpowering of ethical values by personal desires, sets the stage for his eventual downfall. Ravana's journey is a compelling narrative on the consequences of deviating from the moral path, serving as a stark warning of the dangers of allowing ego and desire to cloud judgment.

In contrast, characters like Hanuman and Sita, though facing different dilemmas, demonstrate unwavering commitment to their principles. Hanuman's devotion and service, transcending personal safety and comfort, highlight the virtues of loyalty and selflessness. Sita, on the other hand, remains steadfast in her faith and virtue, despite the hardships she endures, embodying the strength and resilience of dharma even in the most trying circumstances.

### Fun Fact

Modern calculations estimate the distance Hanuman leaped to reach Lanka is about 800 miles (approximately 1,287 kilometers). This feat, considered a mix of devotion and supernatural ability, captivates the imagination about the extents of loyalty and courage.

These diverse manifestations of dharma in the Ramayana create a rich path of moral lessons. From Ravana's tragic fall to Hanuman's exemplar devotion, and Sita's enduring faith, the epic explores the myriad ways in which dharma can be upheld or forsaken. Each character's story contributes to a deeper understanding of dharma, revealing its many facets and the profound impact it has on the lives and destinies of those who either embrace or ignore its principles.

---

Fun Fact

The Ramayana has inspired a UNESCO Intangible Cultural Heritage ballet performance in Indonesia, showcasing the epic's vast influence on the arts globally.

---

## Dharma in Modern Contexts: Navigating the Digital World

In the context of the modern digital world, where information can be disseminated widely and rapidly, the principles of dharma take on a new level of significance. The act of sharing information online, a commonplace activity in our daily lives, becomes a potent example of how we can apply the ancient teachings of dharma in a contemporary setting.

Let's consider a scenario that many of us encounter the decision to post a comment, a news article, or a personal update on social media. Guided by the principles of dharma, this action requires more than a mere impulse to share; it calls for a thoughtful consideration of truthfulness, respect, and the potential impact of our words. Just as Rama deliberated the consequences of his actions on his family, kingdom, and his own moral integrity, we too are urged to reflect on how our online communications might affect others and the broader community.

In this digital age, our words have the power to travel far and fast, often remaining indefinitely in the public domain. Thus, the responsibility that comes with this power is immense. Sharing information that is truthful and verified aligns with the

Ramayana's emphasis on honesty and integrity. It means resisting the urge to spread unverified or misleading content, which can be seen as parallel to Rama's commitment to uphold truth at all costs.

Furthermore, being respectful and considerate in our online interactions echoes Rama's compassionate treatment of even those who wronged him. This means engaging in discussions with empathy and avoiding spreading hate or divisiveness. It involves recognizing the diversity of opinions and backgrounds, and choosing words that build rather than destroy, unify rather than divide.

In a world where online platforms can often become battlegrounds of misinformation and conflict, applying the principles of dharma invites us to create a more thoughtful, truthful, and harmonious digital environment. It challenges us to use our digital presence to foster understanding and goodwill, much like Rama used his influence to uphold dharma and harmony in his realm. By doing so, we not only contribute positively to our online communities but also honor the timeless values of the Ramayana in our contemporary world.

---

### Fun Fact

The Ramayana inspires the world's largest annual drama performance in Bhadrachalam, India, attracting over 300,000 attendees, highlighting the epic's enduring popularity and cultural importance.

---

## The Role of Communities in Upholding Dharma

The concept of creating ethical communities, as reflected in the Ramayana through the thriving kingdom of Ayodhya under Rama's principled rule, has profound implications in our contemporary world. Ayodhya, under Rama's reign, was not just a kingdom of prosperity and peace but also a symbol of a society deeply rooted in the principles of dharma. The citizens of Ayodhya lived in harmony, guided by their leader's commitment to righteousness and justice. This historical portrayal offers a powerful lesson in the importance of cultivating similar ethical communities in our own lives.

In the modern context, these communities can take various forms. Professional networks, for example, can be spaces where individuals commit to conducting business with integrity, transparency, and fairness. These networks can foster environments where ethical dilemmas are discussed openly, and members hold each other accountable to high standards of professional conduct. They can serve as platforms for sharing best practices, mentoring others in ethical decision-making, and creating a ripple effect of integrity in the wider business community.

Similarly, our social circles, including friends and family, can be nurtured as communities where honesty, mutual respect, and support are the bedrock of relationships. In such circles, individuals can find a safe space to discuss personal moral dilemmas, receive guidance, and be encouraged to act in alignment with their principles. The support and understanding from these groups can provide the strength needed to make difficult decisions that adhere to one's ethical beliefs.

Online forums and communities also have the potential to be powerful spaces for reinforcing dharma. These digital platforms can allow for the exchange of diverse viewpoints, encouragement of positive discourse, and the formation of global communities united by shared values of respect and integrity. They can be instrumental in spreading awareness about ethical living and inspiring collective action for social and environmental causes.

By actively participating in and contributing to these ethical communities, we emulate the ideals of Rama's Ayodhya in our contemporary world. These communities provide us not only with a framework for upholding dharma but also reinforce our resolve to navigate life's challenges with moral courage and integrity. They remind us that just as Ayodhya thrived under Rama's rule, our lives, too, can be enriched and fulfilled when we surround ourselves with environments that support and echo our commitment to living a dharmic life.

## Tools and Strategies: Implementing Dharma in Daily Life

Implementing the principles of dharma in daily life can be challenging, especially when faced with complex decisions and ethical dilemmas. To navigate these situations effectively, certain tools and strategies can be employed to ensure that our actions align with the principles of dharma. Two particularly effective tools are the "5 Whys" Technique and the Universal Values Checklist.

1. **The "5 Whys" Technique:** Originally developed for problem-solving in a business context, this technique can be a powerful tool for personal introspection and ethical decision-making. It involves asking the question "Why?" five times in succession to get to the root cause of a particular decision or action. For instance, if faced with a choice that seems to compromise your values, asking "Why?" repeatedly helps peel back the layers of your reasoning, revealing whether the decision is driven by short-term gain, peer pressure, or a genuine alignment with your core values. This method encourages deep reflection and can help clarify whether a particular course of action upholds the principles of dharma, such as truthfulness, righteousness, and consideration for others.

***Example from the Ramayana: Rama's Decision to Go into Exile***

**Situation:** Rama, the crown prince of Ayodhya, is suddenly faced with the decision to go into exile for 14 years, just as he is about to be crowned king.

Application of the "5 Whys" Technique:

1. **Why must Rama go into exile?** - Because his father, King Dasharatha, has to fulfill a promise made to Rama's stepmother, Kaikeyi, who wishes for her son Bharata to become king.

2. **Why does Dasharatha have to fulfill this promise?** - Because he is bound by the principle of dharma, which holds that a promise, once given, must be honored, regardless of its consequences.

3. **Why is upholding this promise so important?** - Upholding promises is crucial because it maintains the moral and ethical order, which is the foundation of righteous governance and personal integrity in the Ramayana.

4. **Why does maintaining moral and ethical order matter?** - It matters because it ensures the wellbeing of society and upholds the principles of justice and righteousness, key tenets of dharma.

5. **Why is Rama willing to adhere to this principle?** - Rama believes in setting an example of self-sacrifice and adherence to dharma, valuing the greater good and moral integrity over personal desires or comfort.

Through this process, it becomes clear that Rama's decision to go into exile, though personally challenging, is deeply aligned with his commitment to dharma, prioritizing the wellbeing and moral order of the kingdom over his own rights and desires.

### *Modern-Day Example: A Business Ethics Dilemma*

**Situation:** A manager in a company is offered a lucrative opportunity to engage in a business deal that promises significant profits but involves some deceptive practices.

Application of the "5 Whys" Technique:

1. **Why consider this business deal?** - Because it offers substantial financial gain for the company.

2. **Why is financial gain important here?** - It can lead to business growth, higher bonuses, and possibly promotions.

3. **Why pursue growth and promotions in this manner?** - Because they are often seen as indicators of success in the corporate world.

4. **Why value these indicators of success?** - They are perceived as ways to achieve personal and professional fulfillment and respect.

5. **Why seek fulfillment and respect through potentially unethical means?** - This question reveals a potential misalignment with personal and organizational values of integrity and honesty. It prompts reconsideration of whether compromising ethical standards is worth the temporary gains, challenging the individual to weigh short-term benefits against long-term values and reputation.

In this modern context, the "5 Whys" technique helps the manager realize that the decision, though beneficial in the short term, conflicts with deeper values of honesty and integrity. It encourages a decision that aligns with ethical business practices, reflecting a commitment to contemporary dharma.

2. **Universal Values Checklist:** This is a practical tool that involves creating a checklist of universal ethical values such as honesty, fairness, empathy, and responsibility. Before making a decision, you can refer to this checklist to assess whether your potential actions align with these values. For example, if contemplating a business decision, you might ask yourself: "Is this honest? Is it fair to all parties involved? Does it demonstrate empathy towards those affected?" By systematically evaluating your choices against these values, you can ensure that your decisions resonate with the ethos of dharma. This checklist not only serves as a guide for individual decisions but also as a benchmark for evaluating ongoing behaviors and practices in your personal and professional life.

### *Example from the Ramayana: Sita's Test of Fire*

***Situation:*** After being rescued from Ravana, Sita is asked to undergo a test of fire to prove her purity and faithfulness to Rama.

Application of the Universal Values Checklist:

- **Honesty:** Sita's decision to undergo the test is a declaration of her truthfulness. She knows her own integrity and wants to demonstrate it openly.

- **Fairness:** The demand for the test raises questions about fairness. Sita's willingness to submit to it can be seen as her commitment to upholding societal norms and values, even at great personal cost.

- **Empathy:** Sita's decision demonstrates empathy for Rama's position as a king who must consider public perception and the societal values of the time.

- **Responsibility:** Sita understands her role as a queen and the expectations placed upon her. Her decision to undergo the test, despite its personal unfairness, reflects her responsibility towards upholding societal norms and her duties as a queen.

This checklist helps illustrate that Sita's decision, while complex and fraught with emotional pain, aligns with the values of honesty, empathy, and responsibility, even as it questions the fairness of the demand placed upon her.

***Modern-Day Example: A Manager's Hiring Decision***

***Situation:*** A manager has to decide between two job candidates: one who is highly qualified but has a history of being difficult to work with, and another who is less qualified but known for a collaborative and positive attitude.

Application of the Universal Values Checklist:

- **Honesty:** The manager must honestly assess not only the qualifications of each candidate but also their potential impact on the team.

- **Fairness:** It's crucial to consider which candidate would be fair to both the needs of the company and the dynamics of the existing team. Would choosing the more skilled candidate be fair if it disrupts team harmony?

- **Empathy:** Understanding the candidates' backgrounds and motivations is essential. How would each candidate fit into the team, and how would their hiring affect current team members?

- **Responsibility:**   The manager has a responsibility to the company for its success and to the team for maintaining a positive and productive work environment.

By using the Universal Values Checklist, the manager can make a more rounded decision, considering not just the immediate needs of the role but the long-term implications for the team and company culture. This approach ensures that the decision is aligned with a broader perspective of ethical and moral responsibility, akin to the principles of dharma.

Both these tools encourage a mindful approach to decision-making, echoing the thoughtful and intentional actions of characters like Rama in the Ramayana. By regularly employing these strategies, we can cultivate a habit of making decisions that are not only beneficial to us but also aligned with the greater good, reflecting the essence of dharma in our daily lives.

## Ramayana's Teachings:   Quotes   and   Real-Life Applications

The Ramayana is replete with profound quotations that encapsulate the essence of dharma and provide guidance for myriad life situations. One of the most impactful teachings is Rama's assertion of duty over personal desire, which serves as a guiding principle for living a life of integrity and righteousness.

*Rama's Quote:*   "My honor is my life; both grow in one; Take honor from me, and my life is done." This statement by Rama reflects the deep intertwining of personal honor with the adherence to one's duty. It highlights that true honor and self-respect are rooted in living a life aligned with one's principles and responsibilities.

## Application in the Workplace

In a professional setting, this teaching can be particularly relevant in situations of conflict or ethical dilemmas. For instance, consider a scenario where a team member is pressured to manipulate data to make a project appear more successful. Rama's emphasis on honor and duty would inspire this individual to uphold integrity, even if it means facing short-term setbacks or challenges. The choice to present accurate data, despite potential repercussions, aligns with the principle of putting duty – in this case, honesty and responsibility – above personal or immediate gains.

## Application in Personal Relationships

In personal relationships, this principle can guide actions and decisions that prioritize collective well-being and ethical standards over individual desires. For example, if someone faces a choice between doing what is easy (such as telling a white lie to avoid conflict) and what is right (such as having a difficult but honest conversation), Rama's teaching would encourage choosing the path of honesty and integrity. This approach not only fosters trust and respect in relationships but also strengthens one's moral character.

## Broader Implications

The teachings of the Ramayana, particularly the emphasis on duty and honor as exemplified by Rama, offer timeless wisdom that can be applied in various aspects of modern life. Whether navigating complex challenges in the workplace, making decisions that affect personal relationships, or facing societal dilemmas, these teachings provide a moral compass.

They remind us that the true measure of success and fulfillment lies not in external achievements or recognition but in living a life that is true to one's principles and duties – a life of dharma.

## Interactive Engagement: Personal Reflection

Interactive engagement through personal reflection is a vital aspect of understanding and integrating the principles of dharma into our lives. It encourages us not just to learn about these concepts but to internalize them through our experiences.

Consider a time in your life when you stood at an ethical crossroads, a moment when your values were tested, and you had to make a choice that defined your character. Perhaps it was a situation at work where you had to decide whether to report a colleague's minor misconduct, or a moment in your personal life where honesty could potentially hurt someone you care about.

Think about how you responded in that situation. Did you choose the path of least resistance, or did you stand by your principles? How did this decision align with the principles of dharma such as truthfulness, righteousness, and doing no harm? Did you consider the greater good, or were your actions driven by personal benefit or fear?

Now, reimagine this scenario through the lens of dharma. How might your decision have been different if you had prioritized these ancient principles? Would you have been more courageous in your honesty, more compassionate in your approach, or more committed to justice? Consider the potential outcomes of this alternate decision. How would it have affected you and the others involved? Would it have led to a more positive or harmonious outcome?

This exercise of reflection is not about regret but about learning and growth. It's about understanding the profound impact our choices have on our lives and the lives of others. By contemplating our past decisions through the principles of dharma, we can gain insights into our own values and motivations. This introspection not only fosters a deeper personal connection with the concept of dharma but also guides us in making more conscious and ethically sound decisions in the future. It reminds us that each choice we make is an opportunity to live a life aligned with our highest principles, echoing the timeless wisdom of the Ramayana.

## The Emotional Resonance of Dharma

The exploration of dharma, as depicted in the Ramayana, transcends mere intellectual understanding; it is an emotional odyssey that delves deep into the essence of living a righteous and purposeful life. This ancient epic does not just narrate stories; it stirs the soul, provoking us to examine the very core of our being and the values we uphold.

As we reach the conclusion of this chapter, it's essential to pause and introspect. Consider the myriad of choices that confront us daily in this complex world. Each decision, whether big or small, shapes the course of our lives. The wisdom of dharma, as exemplified by the characters in the Ramayana, provides a beacon to guide us through these choices. It prompts us to ponder: If we were to consistently apply the principles of dharma in our lives, how would our paths transform? Imagine the profound impact of living with unwavering integrity, making decisions that are not just beneficial for us personally but also contribute positively to those around us and the broader world.

This journey with dharma is not just about making the right decisions; it's about cultivating a legacy. It's about how our actions resonate with and influence others. By embodying the principles of dharma – truthfulness, duty, righteousness, and compassion – we create ripples that extend beyond our immediate environment. We forge a legacy of integrity, a story of life that inspires and uplifts.

Furthermore, this call to dharma, echoing from the verses of the Ramayana, is a call to personal evolution. It invites us to transform ourselves, to rise above our limitations and fears, and to embrace a higher standard of living. It challenges us to look beyond the superficiality of material success and to seek fulfillment in ethical and moral growth.

As we reflect upon the teachings of the Ramayana and the concept of dharma, let us consider how these timeless principles can be woven into the fabric of our daily lives. How can we, in each moment and decision, honor this ancient wisdom? How can our lives become a testament to the enduring power and relevance of dharma?

In embracing these principles, we do more than live; we illuminate a path of righteousness for ourselves and for those who follow. This is the emotional resonance of dharma – a profound and transformative journey that shapes not only our destiny but also the legacy we leave behind.

# Chapter 3

# Leadership Lessons from Lord Rama

---

Fun Fact

Lord Rama's name itself is significant, with "Ra" meaning light and "Ma" meaning within me, in Sanskrit, symbolizing the inner light that dispels spiritual darkness. Additionally, Rama has many other names, such as 'Ramachandra' (moon-like gentle Rama), indicating his compassionate nature and serene beauty.

---

In the intricate world of modern leadership, where decision-makers like CEOs are frequently confronted with challenging dilemmas that test their ethical boundaries, the ancient wisdom encapsulated in the Ramayana, particularly through the character of Lord Rama, becomes significantly relevant. This epic, revered for centuries, is not just a story but a reservoir of deep philosophical insights. One of its most powerful messages, "When righteousness is weak and faints and unrighteousness exults in pride, then my spirit arises on earth," speaks volumes to leaders in today's fast-paced, often morally ambiguous business environment.

This statement from the Ramayana can be seen as a clarion call for ethical leadership in times when the lines between right and wrong are blurred. For instance, a CEO facing the temptation to cut corners environmentally for profit might find guidance in this adage. It serves as a reminder that true leadership strength emerges when faced with the temptation to forsake moral principles for expedient gains. It encourages leaders to rise above short-term perspectives and prideful gains, advocating for a leadership style that is anchored in righteousness and ethical fortitude.

Fun Fact

Did you know that the Ramayana is not just a single story but has over 300 versions found across different cultures and countries, including Thailand, Cambodia, Indonesia, and even the Philippines? Each version adapts the story to fit local customs and perspectives, highlighting its universal themes of morality, leadership, and righteousness.

The context in which this wisdom was conveyed – an era marked by kings and sages, where dharma (righteous duty) was the cornerstone of governance – might differ vastly from today's corporate world. However, the essence of these teachings remains timeless. They urge today's leaders to introspect and consider the wider impact of their decisions, not just on their immediate stakeholders but on the environment, society, and future generations.

Thus, in a landscape marked by complexities such as balancing profit motives with sustainable practices, addressing stakeholder expectations ethically, and leading organizations through turbulent economic and social changes, the ancient wisdom of the Ramayana, particularly the virtues exemplified by Lord Rama, offers a beacon of guidance. It inspires modern leaders to navigate their roles with a sense of moral responsibility, integrity, and a vision that transcends the immediate gains, aligning with the deeper, enduring values of righteousness and ethical leadership.

## Rama's Leadership within Historical and Cultural Context

In the vast and rich landscape of Hindu mythology, Lord Rama stands as a pivotal figure, not only for his heroic deeds but also for his exemplary leadership qualities. Rooted deeply in the principle of dharma, or righteous duty, Rama's approach to leadership offers profound insights that transcend the boundaries of time and culture, making them highly relevant to contemporary leadership challenges.

Rama's leadership is characterized by a steadfast adherence to dharma, which in the context of the Ramayana, goes beyond mere duty. It encompasses a broader spectrum of righteousness, moral integrity, and ethical responsibility. His life, as depicted in the epic, presents a series of challenging scenarios where his commitment to dharma is tested, from the decision to honor his father's promise and go into exile to his handling of complex situations in the forest and his eventual battle against Ravana.

Fun Fact

Lord Rama is also worshipped as a deity in Jainism but with a different narrative. In Jain texts, Rama is considered a righteous king who achieves liberation (moksha) through non-violence (ahimsa) and truth, showcasing the cross-religious influence of his character and the diverse interpretations of dharma.

In each of these instances, Rama demonstrates qualities that form the bedrock of strong and principled leadership. His actions reflect not just a duty to uphold personal honor, but a deeper commitment to the welfare of others, be it his family, his subjects, or even the entire realm of nature and society he interacts with. This holistic approach to leadership, where decisions are made considering the impact on all stakeholders, is particularly relevant in today's world, where leaders are often required to navigate complex ethical landscapes.

Moreover, Rama's leadership is marked by a compassionate understanding of others' perspectives, an essential quality in any leader. His interactions with various characters in the Ramayana, from his loyal brother Lakshmana to the devoted Hanuman and even his adversaries, are characterized by empathy, respect, and an understanding of their unique viewpoints and circumstances. This empathetic approach, combined with a strong moral compass, positions Rama as a leader who not only achieves his goals but does so with a sense of ethical responsibility and kindness.

In the historical and cultural context of Hindu mythology, where kings were expected to be the upholders of dharma, Rama's story serves as a guiding light. For modern leaders, his approach offers valuable lessons in balancing the often competing demands of leading with authority while maintaining moral integrity, showing empathy and understanding towards others, and making decisions that are ethically sound and beneficial for the greater good. This ancient narrative, therefore, holds significant contemporary relevance, offering a framework for leadership that is as robust and effective today as it was in the mythical era of the Ramayana.

## Rama's Interactions and Leadership Dynamics

Rama's leadership style, as depicted through his interactions with pivotal characters in the Ramayana, offers deep insights into the essence of effective and empathetic leadership. These interactions underscore the value of interpersonal dynamics and strategic collaboration in leadership roles:

1. **Learning from Lakshmana**: Rama's bond with his brother Lakshmana was founded on deep mutual respect and trust. Lakshmana's unwavering loyalty and support were met with Rama's acknowledgment and appreciation of his brother's sacrifices and opinions. This relationship exemplifies the importance of acknowledging and valuing the contributions of team members. In a modern context, this dynamic translates into leaders fostering a culture of mutual respect, actively seeking input from their teams, and recognizing their efforts, thereby creating a loyal and committed workforce.

   *Example in a Corporate Setting:*

   *Situation:* Sarah, a team leader at a tech company, faces a critical project deadline. Her team is diverse, with varying levels of experience and expertise.

   *Learning from Lakshmana:* Just as Rama valued Lakshmana's loyalty and insights, Sarah recognizes the importance of each team member's contribution. She is particularly aware of one team member, Alex, who is relatively new but has shown great enthusiasm and innovative thinking.

   *Application:*

   *Actively Seeking Input:* During a team meeting, Sarah openly asks for ideas on how to tackle the project's challenges. When Alex proposes a novel approach that differs from the standard procedure, instead of dismissing it due to his inexperience, Sarah encourages him to elaborate. This mirrors Rama's approach with

Lakshmana, where he would consider his brother's viewpoints seriously, fostering a sense of mutual respect and inclusion.

***Acknowledging Contributions:*** As the project progresses, Sarah makes it a point to acknowledge and appreciate Alex's innovative ideas, which significantly contribute to the project's success. She highlights his contributions in front of the entire team and credits him for his role in the project's successful completion.

***Building Loyalty and Commitment:*** This approach not only boosts Alex's confidence and loyalty to the team but also sets an example for the entire team about the value of each member's input and the culture of mutual respect. It fosters an environment where team members feel valued and, therefore, are more committed and engaged.

In this scenario, just as Lakshmana's dedication and support were crucial to Rama's success, Alex's contributions become pivotal to the project's success under Sarah's leadership. By emulating Rama's respectful and inclusive treatment of Lakshmana, Sarah enhances team cohesion, drives innovation, and strengthens loyalty within her team. This approach is a powerful example of how ancient wisdom can be applied to modern-day leadership to create a positive and productive work environment.

2. **Empowerment of Hanuman:** Rama's interaction with Hanuman is a prime example of empowering leadership. Rama saw potential in Hanuman and entrusted him with critical tasks, like the search for Sita. This trust and empowerment led Hanuman to achieve feats beyond his

perceived capabilities. In contemporary leadership, this mirrors the practice of empowering employees, which can lead to increased innovation, engagement, and performance. By entrusting team members with significant responsibilities and expressing confidence in their abilities, leaders can unlock their potential, much like Rama did with Hanuman.

---

Fun Fact

Hanuman is also considered a master of grammar and linguistics! In fact, he is said to have learned all the languages of the world in just one day.

---

***Example in a Marketing Team:***

***Situation:*** Emily, the head of a marketing department in a mid-sized company, is facing a challenging campaign with tight deadlines and high stakes for the company's growth.

***Empowerment of Hanuman:*** Emily recognizes the potential in a junior team member, Mark, who has shown creativity and a fresh perspective in previous minor projects but has never led a major campaign.

***Application:***

***Entrusting with Critical Tasks:*** Drawing inspiration from Rama's empowerment of Hanuman, Emily decides to give Mark the lead role in developing a key segment of the campaign. She communicates her decision to the team, highlighting her trust in Mark's abilities and potential, similar to how Rama entrusted significant responsibilities to Hanuman.

***Providing Support and Guidance:*** While she assigns Mark this significant responsibility, Emily also ensures he has access to the necessary resources and mentorship. She regularly checks in with him, offering guidance and support, but also gives him the autonomy to make key decisions. This approach mirrors Rama's way of empowering Hanuman, giving him the freedom to use his abilities to their fullest potential.

***Unlocking Potential and Achieving Success:*** Empowered by this trust and responsibility, Mark brings innovative ideas to the campaign and works diligently to execute them effectively. His fresh approach and creativity lead to the campaign's notable success, surpassing the company's expectations.

***Positive Ripple Effect:*** This success not only boosts Mark's confidence and career growth but also inspires his colleagues. It fosters a culture where innovation is encouraged, and team members feel valued and empowered to take initiative.

In this example, just like Hanuman's empowered role led to the successful search for Sita, Mark's empowered position leads to a successful campaign. Emily's leadership approach, inspired by Rama's empowerment of Hanuman, demonstrates the effectiveness of entrusting team members with significant responsibilities and fostering an environment where their potential can be fully realized. This modern parallel shows how ancient leadership lessons can be effectively applied in contemporary settings to enhance team performance and innovation.

3. **Strategic Alliance with Sugriva:** Rama's alliance with Sugriva, the king of the Vanaras, demonstrates strategic acumen and the ability to build beneficial partnerships.

Their alliance was based on understanding each other's needs and working together towards a common goal: Rama helped Sugriva regain his kingdom, and in return, Sugriva aided Rama in his quest to rescue Sita. This illustrates the importance of strategic networking and collaboration in leadership. Modern leaders can learn from this by building alliances and partnerships that are mutually beneficial, ensuring a collaborative approach to achieving common objectives.

---

Fun Fact

Sugriva's kingdom, Kishkindha, is associated with the real-life Hampi in Karnataka, India, known for its stunning ancient ruins and landscapes.

---

### Example in the Business World:

**Situation:** Jennifer, the CEO of a burgeoning tech startup, is looking to expand her company's market reach. However, she faces challenges in terms of resources and industry connections.

**Strategic Alliance with Sugriva:** Drawing inspiration from Rama's strategic alliance with Sugriva, Jennifer identifies an opportunity to collaborate with another company, GreenTech Innovations, which specializes in eco-friendly technology and has a strong market presence but lacks innovative software solutions, which Jennifer's company excels in.

### Application:

**Understanding Mutual Needs:** Just as Rama and Sugriva assessed each other's needs and capabilities, Jennifer and the CEO of GreenTech, David, meet to discuss potential synergies. They realize that a partnership could be mutually beneficial: Jennifer's company can provide innovative software to enhance GreenTech's products, while GreenTech can offer a broader market reach and industry expertise.

***Forming a Beneficial Partnership:*** They agree to a strategic partnership where Jennifer's company will develop custom software solutions for GreenTech's products. In return, GreenTech will integrate these solutions into their products, providing Jennifer's company with exposure to a wider customer base.

***Working Towards Common Goals:*** The alliance proves to be successful. GreenTech's products, enhanced with Jennifer's innovative software, receive a significant boost in the market, while Jennifer's company benefits from increased visibility and revenue. Both companies work closely on product development, marketing strategies, and customer outreach, ensuring alignment of goals and strategies.

***Long-Term Collaboration:*** The partnership evolves into a long-term collaboration, leading to sustained growth for both companies. This mirrors the successful alliance between Rama and Sugriva, where both parties achieved their objectives through mutual support and cooperation.

In this example, Jennifer's strategic alliance with GreenTech mirrors the alliance between Rama and Sugriva in the Ramayana. It highlights the importance of understanding mutual needs, forming partnerships based on complementary strengths, and working collaboratively towards shared objectives. This approach to leadership and business strategy demonstrates how ancient wisdom can be applied to modern business challenges, fostering success through strategic networking and collaboration.

Each of these interactions from the Ramayana not only highlights different aspects of Rama's leadership style but also provides valuable lessons for modern-day leaders. By understanding and implementing these dynamics, leaders can enhance their interpersonal skills, foster stronger teams, and build effective partnerships, all of which are essential for successful leadership in today's complex and interconnected world.

## Application of Rama's Qualities in Contemporary Leadership

The application of Lord Rama's leadership qualities in contemporary settings offers a blueprint for modern leaders to navigate through various challenges with integrity and effectiveness:

1. **Empathy and Compassion**: When undergoing organizational changes, such as restructuring or downsizing, a leader's role becomes crucial in managing the process with sensitivity and empathy. By emulating Rama's empathetic approach, leaders can ensure transparent communication, provide support systems for affected employees, and seek to minimize negative impacts, much like how Rama cared for the welfare of every individual in his kingdom.

---

### Fun Fact

There's a heartwarming tale about a small squirrel who helped Rama build the bridge to Lanka. The story highlights Rama's appreciation for even the smallest contributions towards a greater cause. Rama gently stroked the squirrel's back with his fingers, leaving the stripes that squirrels have to this day, according to this legend.

2. **Integrity and Moral Fortitude**:  In situations of ethical dilemmas, such as corporate espionage or insider trading, embodying Rama's integrity becomes essential. Leaders faced with these challenges can draw from Rama's unwavering commitment to righteousness, choosing to uphold ethical standards and maintain transparency, thus building trust and credibility within and outside their organizations.

3. **Inclusivity and Team Building**: Rama's ability to embrace diverse perspectives and foster unity is crucial in today's globalized work environment. Leaders can create an inclusive culture by actively encouraging diverse voices, facilitating collaborative teamwork, and leveraging the varied strengths and skills of team members, just as Rama did with his diverse coalition of allies.

4. **Decision Making with Discernment**: In complex scenarios, such as mergers, acquisitions, or entering new markets, leaders can adopt Rama's approach of thoughtful and discerning decision-making. This involves carefully evaluating the implications of each decision, considering both the short-term and long-term impact on stakeholders, and aligning decisions with the organization's core values and ethical principles.

   - **Decision to Leave Ayodhya for Exile:**  Rama's choice to honor his father's promise and go into exile, forsaking his right to the throne.

   - **Not Taking Revenge on Ravana Immediately After Sita's Rescue:** Rama's decision to offer Ravana a chance to amend his ways instead of seeking immediate revenge after rescuing Sita.

These historical examples from the Ramayana highlight Rama's ability to make thoughtful decisions that consider the greater good and ethical principles, serving as powerful references for modern leaders facing complex decision-making scenarios.

5. **Resilience and Adaptability**: Facing challenges such as market volatility, technological disruptions, or crises, leaders can look to Rama's example during his exile and battles. His resilience in adversity and ability to adapt to changing circumstances while staying true to his mission are qualities that leaders can emulate to navigate through uncertain times while keeping their teams focused and motivated.

6. **Vision and Purpose**:   Rama's clear vision for the welfare of his kingdom reflects the importance of leading with a purpose that goes beyond mere profitability. Modern leaders can be inspired by this to align their organizational goals with broader ethical and societal values, ensuring their business practices contribute positively to the community and environment, thus achieving sustainable success.

By integrating these qualities exemplified by Rama, contemporary leaders can not only enhance their leadership effectiveness but also drive their organizations towards ethical excellence and sustainable growth. These principles provide a comprehensive framework for leading

in today's dynamic and often challenging business landscape, ensuring decisions and actions are not only beneficial for the organization but also resonate with higher ethical and moral standards. This approach to leadership, rooted in ancient wisdom yet profoundly relevant in the modern context, encourages leaders to create a positive impact on their teams, organizations, and society at large.

## Modern Challenges and a Case Study

In the contemporary business landscape, leaders often confront challenges like technological disruptions and political polarization. These situations test the ethical boundaries and decision-making skills of even the most seasoned leaders. The principles exemplified by Lord Rama provide a valuable compass for navigating such challenges with integrity and foresight.

### Modern Challenges

- **Technological Disruptions:** The rapid pace of technological change can lead to ethical dilemmas, particularly in areas like data privacy, artificial intelligence, and automation. Rama's qualities, such as discernment and commitment to dharma (righteous duty), can guide leaders in making decisions that balance innovation with ethical implications, ensuring that technological advancements serve the greater good without compromising ethical standards.

- **Political Polarization:** In an era marked by increasing political divides, a leader's ability to foster unity and understanding is crucial. Rama's approach to leadership, characterized by empathy, inclusivity, and a focus on the common good, can inspire leaders to bridge divides, create dialogues, and build cohesive environments, both within their organizations and in their wider communities.

### Case Study: Prioritizing User Privacy in the Tech Industry

Consider the case of a tech CEO, Alex, at the helm of a growing analytics company. Alex is faced with a decision: to monetize user data for higher profits, a common practice in the industry, or to prioritize user privacy, even at the expense of immediate financial gains.

- ***The Decision:*** Embodying Rama's principles, Alex chooses to prioritize user privacy. This decision involves implementing stringent data protection policies, transparent communication with users about data usage, and investing in secure data practices.

- ***Implementation and Challenges:*** Alex faces initial pushback internally and skepticism from stakeholders about the profitability of this ethical stance. However, consistent with Rama's resilience and adaptability, Alex remains steadfast in his decision, focusing on long-term trust and ethical practices.

- ***Outcomes:***  Over time, this decision earns the company a reputation for integrity and reliability. As public awareness and concern about data privacy grow, the company emerges as a leader in ethical data practices. This results in increased user trust, brand loyalty, and ultimately, sustainable growth and profitability.

- ***Broader Impact:*** Alex's decision not only sets a new standard in the industry but also influences other companies to reconsider their data policies. The company's commitment to ethical practices in a technologically driven environment resonates with Rama's dedication to righteousness, demonstrating how ethical leadership can lead to success and drive positive change in the industry.

This case study exemplifies how the application of Rama's leadership qualities to modern business challenges can yield significant benefits. By prioritizing ethical considerations over short-term gains, leaders like Alex can navigate the complexities of technological advancements and political polarization, creating a legacy of trust, integrity, and ethical business practices. The approach not only aligns with the higher principles of leadership demonstrated by Rama but also addresses the demands and expectations of a contemporary audience, showing that ethical leadership is not only morally right but also strategically sound in today's business world.

## Interactive Elements for Deeper Engagement

To enhance deeper engagement and personal application of the leadership lessons derived from Lord Rama's character, interactive elements can be incorporated into the learning process. These elements are designed to encourage introspection and self-assessment, allowing individuals to reflect on their own leadership styles in relation to the qualities exemplified by Rama.

### *Self-Reflection Questions*

1. **Analyzing Past Decisions**:  Think of a challenging decision you had to make in a leadership role. Reflect on how you approached this decision. How might applying Rama's qualities of empathy, integrity, and discernment have altered the process or outcome?

2. **Handling Conflicts**:  Recall a conflict situation within your team or organization. Consider Rama's approach to conflict resolution, marked by empathy and inclusivity. How could these qualities have impacted the resolution of your conflict?

3. **Navigating Ethical Dilemmas**:  Reflect on a time when you faced an ethical dilemma in your leadership journey. How did you resolve it? Consider Rama's unwavering commitment to

ethical principles. How might aligning with these principles have influenced your decision-making process?

### Leadership Assessment

1. **Comparing Qualities**:   Evaluate your leadership style against key qualities of Rama such as empathy, integrity, inclusivity, strategic decision-making, resilience, and a clear vision. Which of these qualities do you consistently demonstrate? Where do you see room for improvement?

2. **Identifying Development Areas**:   Based on this comparison, identify specific areas where you can develop further. For instance, if you find a gap in empathetic leadership, consider strategies to enhance your emotional intelligence and understanding of team dynamics.

3. **Action Plan for Growth**:   Create a personalized action plan to develop the identified areas. This could involve mentorship, training, reading, or practical exercises designed to cultivate specific qualities. Set measurable goals to track your progress in embodying these leadership traits.

By engaging with these interactive elements, leaders can gain a deeper understanding of how ancient wisdom can be applied in modern contexts. This introspective process encourages not just the acquisition of knowledge, but also its practical application, leading to personal growth and enhanced leadership effectiveness.

## Embracing Rama's Leadership Philosophy

Embracing Lord Rama's leadership philosophy indeed has the potential to initiate a significant cultural shift within organizations, a change that is both profound and impactful. When leaders start embodying Rama's qualities such as empathy, integrity, and visionary leadership, it sets a powerful example for others in leadership positions, leading to a transformative shift in organizational culture.

1. **Influence on Other Leaders**: Leaders who demonstrate empathetic and ethical leadership serve as role models within their organizations. This influence is particularly potent in hierarchical structures where leadership styles and attitudes tend to cascade down the ranks. As more leaders within the organization begin to observe and emulate these qualities, it creates a domino effect, gradually transforming the overall leadership approach across the organization.

2. **Shift in Organizational Values**: When the top leadership starts prioritizing ethical practices and inclusive policies, these values become ingrained in the organization's ethos. This shift often leads to revising policies, redefining success metrics, and restructuring systems to align with these newly emphasized values. As a result, the organization starts to value not just profitability but also the welfare of its employees, the impact on the community, and the sustainability of its practices.

3. **Creating a Ripple Effect in the Workforce**: As leaders at different levels start to embody Rama's qualities, employees at all levels begin to experience a more inclusive, empathetic, and principled work environment. This experience can significantly enhance employee satisfaction, loyalty, and productivity. Moreover, it fosters an environment where employees feel valued and empowered, encouraging them to take initiative and be innovative, further contributing to the organization's success.

4. **Long-Term Cultural Transformation**: Over time, this shift in leadership style and organizational values leads to a long-term cultural transformation. An organization that

once might have operated on purely transactional or profit-driven motives evolves into one that values ethical decision-making, employee well-being, and social responsibility. This transformation goes beyond superficial changes; it becomes a part of the organization's identity, attracting like-minded talent and customers who share similar values.

5. **Impact Beyond the Organization**: Organizations that undergo this cultural shift can also influence their industry and the broader business community. As they set new standards for ethical leadership and social responsibility, they may inspire other organizations to follow suit, leading to a wider societal impact.

By embodying the leadership philosophy of Lord Rama, leaders can be the catalysts for a positive and enduring change within their organizations. This transformation in leadership ethos and organizational culture aligns not just with achieving business success but also with fulfilling a greater societal role. It's a journey towards building organizations that are not only successful in traditional terms but are also pillars of ethical practices and positive social impact. This chapter, therefore, is an invitation to leaders to embark on a transformative journey, one that uses the guiding principles of Rama's leadership to navigate modern challenges and build a legacy that is ethical, impactful, and enduring.

# Chapter 4

# Sita: Resilience and Inner Strength

In the heart of the Ramayana, the story of Sita emerges as a profound example of resilience and inner strength. Set against the backdrop of ancient India, her journey is a compelling narrative of endurance, grace, and an unwavering spirit, offering timeless lessons in overcoming adversity with dignity. From her early life in Mithila to her challenging days in Lanka, Sita's experiences weave a tale of contrast, resilience, and deep-rooted strength. As she once declared, "I am the daughter of the Earth, strong and unyielding. I will not be shaken by adversity." This quote eloquently sets the stage for understanding Sita's character—a personification of resilience and steadfastness, firmly rooted in her unshakeable strength.

Fun Fact

Mithila, Sita's birthplace, is also renowned for its unique form of painting known as Madhubani. This art form, which dates back to the time of the Ramayana, is traditionally done by women of the region and features intricate patterns and vibrant colors that tell tales of folklore, including Sita's own story.

One of the most striking instances of Sita's resilience is seen during her captivity in Lanka. Despite being in the clutches of

Ravana, she refuses to surrender her devotion to Rama. Her defiance against Ravana's advances, maintaining her vow of faithfulness to Rama, is a testament to her unyielding strength and determination. Facing immense pressure and temptation, Sita's moral fortitude and steadfast character were put to a defining test. It was during her trial by fire, a moment both literal and metaphorical, that Sita's resilience shone brightest. Confronted with the fiery ordeal to prove her purity, she stood unwavering, embodying her own truth and integrity. In her own words, she affirmed, "Here I stand, pure and unswayed, in the fire of my own truth." This poignant declaration during her trial underscores not only her commitment to her principles but also her profound inner strength, even in the face of harsh judgment and scrutiny.

Sita's experiences in the Ramayana, though set in a different era, hold significant relevance in today's world. Her ability to withstand and emerge stronger from her trials provides valuable insights for modern individuals facing various challenges. In an age where external pressures and ethical dilemmas are rampant, Sita's story serves as a reminder of the importance of staying true to one's values and beliefs, even in the most challenging circumstances. Her resilience in adversity, her grace under pressure, and her unwavering commitment to her principles resonate powerfully with contemporary themes of personal integrity, moral courage, and the strength of character.

### Fun Fact

It's fascinating to note that Sita's name means "furrow" in Sanskrit, symbolizing fertility and the earth's bounty. According to legend, she was found in a furrow by her father, King Janaka, while he was ploughing the field, emphasizing her connection to the Earth and her embodiment as a daughter of Mother Earth. This origin story highlights her intrinsic link to nature and fertility, underscoring her character as nurturing yet resilient.

## Applying Sita's Resilience in Contemporary Contexts

- **Overcoming Personal Challenges**:  Sita's story encourages individuals facing personal trials, whether they be in relationships, career, or personal growth, to persevere with dignity and strength, maintaining their core values.

- **Leadership and Workplace Challenges**:  In the corporate world, leaders can draw inspiration from Sita's resilience to foster a work environment that values integrity, respects individuality, and encourages overcoming challenges through ethical practices and perseverance.

- **Social and Community Issues**:  Sita's resilience provides a framework for addressing social issues like inequality and injustice. Her example inspires individuals and communities to stand firm in their beliefs and to strive for change with patience and determination.

Sita's narrative in the Ramayana transcends its ancient origins to offer enduring wisdom relevant to our modern lives. Her resilience, showcased in her defiance against Ravana and her unwavering fidelity to Rama, offers lessons in facing life's challenges with grace and integrity. This chapter invites readers to reflect on Sita's story, drawing on her strength and resilience to navigate their own life's challenges. Embracing Sita's legacy is about more than admiring a historical figure; it's about integrating her timeless wisdom into our daily lives to cultivate resilience, integrity, and inner strength in the face of adversity.

## Sita's Story: Vividly Portrayed

Sita's life, spun from the sun-drenched days in Mithila to the desolate shadows of Lanka, unfolds in an era steeped in ancient traditions and societal norms. Her early years in Mithila, a realm fragrant with laughter and bathed in golden light, were governed by expectations typical of women in that historical context. Women were often seen as embodiments of honor and virtue, with their lives largely revolving around domestic roles and familial duties. Yet, Sita transcended these conventions. Her time in exile with Rama marked a departure from palace comforts, where she embraced the austere simplicity of forest life with unwavering love and adaptability, showcasing a strength often unattributed to women of her time.

---

### Fun Fact

In certain narratives, Sita trained in archery and combat alongside Rama and Lakshmana. She even actively participated in battles, showcasing her strength and skill.

---

In Lanka, under Ravana's menacing shadow, Sita's resilience was not just a personal testament but also a subtle defiance against the societal norms that sought to define and confine her. Isolated and threatened, she faced relentless assaults on her integrity. In a culture where a woman's honor was closely tied to her compliance and subservience, Sita's firm stance and moral resilience stood out. She stood as a beacon in a storm-tossed sea, her dignity and endurance under immense pressure challenging the status quo and redefining the strength that lay within women of her era and beyond.

Thus, Sita's dignified endurance and unwavering spirit were not merely personal triumphs but also acts of quiet rebellion against the societal norms of her time. Her story is a testament to the strength that lies dormant within us all, waiting to challenge and transcend the conventions of any era.

## Relatable Lessons from Sita's Life

Though centuries separate us, Sita's experiences resonate powerfully with the struggles of modern individuals. Consider Alice, a young journalist navigating the treacherous currents of today's media landscape. Like Sita in Lanka, Alice grapples with pressures to compromise her ethics for career gain. Alluring headlines whisper promises of success, but Alice, mirroring Sita's unwavering commitment to righteousness, chooses the path of truth, her voice a beacon of integrity even as doubts about missed opportunities gnaw at her.

Adding to Alice's narrative, let's look at David, a healthcare professional faced with the dilemma of adhering to bureaucratic pressures versus prioritizing patient care. In moments where expedience is prized over empathy, David, inspired by Sita's moral fortitude, champions the cause of his patients, reflecting the essence of compassionate and ethical practice.

Similarly, consider Maya, an entrepreneur in the tech industry. In a sector driven by fast profits and competitive edge, Maya stands out by embedding ethical practices and sustainability into her business model. Her commitment to ethical entrepreneurship, even at the cost of slower financial growth, parallels Sita's dedication to righteousness amidst challenging circumstances.

## Addressing Contemporary Challenges

- **Navigating Workplace Discrimination:** Sita's resilience serves as a guiding light for individuals confronting discrimination in their professional lives. Her example encourages them to steadfastly uphold their values and seek fairness, embodying her grace and fortitude in challenging environments.

- **Sita's Trial by Fire:**   After her rescue from Lanka, Sita faced unjust accusations and skepticism regarding her purity and fidelity. Despite her unwavering loyalty to Rama during her abduction, she was subjected to a trial by fire to prove her innocence. This trial was not just a physical challenge but also a societal judgment, reflecting the discrimination she faced even after enduring immense hardships. Sita, with dignity and confidence in her own truth, underwent this trial, emerging unscathed, thus proving her integrity. Her resilience in facing this unjust scrutiny and her grace under such pressure are emblematic of her strength of character.

- **A Modern Workplace Scenario:** Consider Priya, a talented and dedicated employee in a tech company, who consistently delivers exceptional work. However, she finds herself overlooked for promotions and facing subtle biases because of her gender. Like Sita, Priya faces unjust treatment in a professional setting. Drawing inspiration from Sita's resilience, Priya decides to address this discrimination. She gathers evidence of her accomplishments and contributions, presents her case to the management, and advocates for a fair and unbiased evaluation process. Her actions lead to a review of the company's promotion policies and open up a broader conversation about gender equality in the workplace. Priya's stance, much like Sita's, is a powerful example of facing discrimination with dignity and taking proactive steps to challenge and change unfair practices.

- **Environmental Advocacy:** Sita's profound connection to nature and unwavering spirit resonate deeply with those advocating for environmental protection. Her enduring commitment inspires perseverance in environmental efforts, even in the face of daunting setbacks.

- **Sita's Connection to Nature in Exile**:   During her time in exile with Rama, Sita demonstrated a profound bond with the natural world. Living in the forest, she showed deep respect and harmony with the environment, embracing its simplicity and beauty despite the hardships of exile. Her life in the forest was marked by a sustainable and minimalistic lifestyle, showing reverence and care for the natural world around her. This period of her life highlights her understanding of the importance of living in balance with nature.

> Fun Fact
>
> The forests where Sita, Rama, and Lakshmana spent their exile are often associated with the current-day Dandakaranya region, spanning several Indian states. This area is still rich in biodiversity and is home to numerous tribes whose lifestyles and beliefs are deeply intertwined with nature, echoing Sita's respect and harmony with the forest.

- **Modern Environmental Advocacy**:   Consider the story of Anika, an environmental activist working to protect a local forest from deforestation due to commercial development. Inspired by Sita's deep connection with nature and her resilience in facing challenges, Anika leads a grassroots campaign against the deforestation. She organizes community meetings, coordinates peaceful protests, and works tirelessly to raise awareness about the ecological importance of the forest. Like Sita, Anika faces setbacks, including legal challenges and public apathy, but she remains committed to her cause.

Anika's efforts eventually lead to a significant public support movement, drawing attention from national media and environmental organizations. Her unwavering spirit and dedication to protecting the environment mirror Sita's respect and care for the natural world, demonstrating how individual perseverance can mobilize a larger movement for environmental conservation in today's world.

- **Mental Health Struggles**: The importance of inner strength, as highlighted in Sita's story, offers hope and resilience to individuals grappling with mental health challenges. Her journey reflects the power of maintaining mental fortitude and self-belief through difficult times.

  - **Sita's Isolation in Lanka**: During her abduction and subsequent captivity in Lanka, Sita faced extreme isolation and emotional distress. Despite being far from her loved ones and under constant threat from Ravana, she managed to maintain her mental fortitude and self-belief. Sita's strength in these circumstances wasn't just about physical survival; it was deeply rooted in her mental resilience. She held onto hope, her values, and her sense of self, despite the harrowing conditions and the psychological turmoil she endured. This period of her life highlights her remarkable inner strength and her ability to sustain her mental well-being in the face of adversity.

  - **Modern Example of Mental Health Resilience**: Consider the story of Jordan, a young professional facing severe anxiety and depression. Like Sita, Jordan finds himself in a situation that tests his mental endurance. Despite professional success, he feels isolated and struggles with overwhelming stress and self-doubt.

    Inspired by Sita's resilience, Jordan decides to seek help and starts therapy. He learns to practice mindfulness and self-compassion, finding strength in his own journey of self-discovery and healing. Over time, Jordan develops coping mechanisms that help him manage his mental health challenges. His story mirrors Sita's fortitude in Lanka, showing that with support, self-care, and inner strength, it is possible to overcome mental health struggles and emerge stronger.

## Broadening the Scope of Resilience

- **Family Relationships:** Sita's enduring love and loyalty, even in times of separation and misunderstanding, offer insights into maintaining strong familial bonds through life's ups and downs.

  - **Sita's Loyalty During Exile:** When Rama was exiled from Ayodhya, Sita chose to accompany him, leaving behind the comfort and security of the palace. Her decision was rooted in her unwavering love and loyalty to Rama. Despite the hardships of forest life and the uncertainty of their future, Sita remained steadfast in her commitment to Rama. This period in her life was marked by separation from her family and familiar life, yet her devotion and understanding never wavered. Her ability to maintain strong bonds with Rama, even in adverse conditions, highlights her deep commitment to her family relationships.

  - **Modern Example of Family Resilience:** Consider the story of Emma, a woman whose partner, like Sita's husband, Rama, must move abroad for an extended period due to work commitments. Despite the challenges of a long-distance relationship and the pressures of raising their children alone, Emma remains committed to maintaining a strong family bond.

    Emma actively fosters communication between her partner and their children, organizes regular video calls, and creates a supportive environment at home that keeps the essence of their family intact. She also finds ways to manage her own emotional well-being, seeking support from friends and family, much like Sita found strength in her own resolve and beliefs. Emma's dedication and efforts to keep her family connected across distances reflect Sita's loyalty and commitment, illustrating how enduring love and understanding can preserve familial bonds, even through periods of separation and difficulty.

- **Creative Pursuits**: For artists and creatives, Sita's journey inspires persistence in one's passion, much like her unwavering commitment to her ideals despite challenges.

  - **Sita's Strength in Adversity**: During her time in exile and captivity, Sita found solace and strength in her inner world. Despite being removed from her familiar life and facing daunting challenges, she maintained a strong sense of self and purpose. This inner resilience can be likened to a creative force, where she nurtured her beliefs and values, staying true to them against all odds. Her ability to hold onto her ideals and find strength within herself, even in the absence of external support, mirrors the journey of an artist or creative individual who must often draw from their inner resources to stay true to their creative vision.

  - **Modern Creative Resilience**: Consider the story of Leo, a young musician facing rejection and criticism as he tries to establish himself in a highly competitive industry. Like Sita, Leo experiences periods of doubt and isolation, where his creative pursuits are met with challenges and setbacks. However, inspired by Sita's unwavering commitment to her ideals, Leo continues to compose and perform, drawing strength from his passion for music and his belief in his artistic vision.

He spends time refining his skills, exploring new styles, and staying true to his unique voice, even when faced with the temptation to conform to mainstream trends for quicker success. Over time, Leo's persistence pays off as he slowly gains recognition for his authentic and innovative work, much like Sita's enduring commitment to her ideals garnered respect and admiration.

Leo's journey in the arts, fueled by perseverance and a strong belief in his creative vision, mirrors Sita's resilience and steadfastness. It illustrates how, in the realm of creative pursuits, maintaining one's passion and authenticity, even in the face of challenges, can lead to fulfillment and recognition. This parallel demonstrates the timeless relevance of Sita's story, inspiring individuals in the modern world to stay committed to their creative passions despite obstacles.

## Leadership Applications Inspired by Sita

- **Practical Strategies for Resilience**: Leaders can implement resilience-building practices such as mindfulness, ethical decision-making exercises, and empathy training, drawing inspiration from Sita's qualities.

- **Sita's Resilience**: Sita was the wife of Rama, the prince of Ayodhya. When Rama was exiled for 14 years, Sita chose to accompany him into the forest. During their exile, they faced many challenges, including kidnapping, violence, and natural disasters. Despite these challenges, Sita remained hopeful and optimistic. She supported Rama and helped him to maintain his strength and determination.

- **Modern Example of Resilience**: A modern-day example of resilience can be found in the story of Malala Yousafzai. Malala is a Pakistani activist who was shot by the Taliban in 2012 for advocating for girls' education. After being shot, Malala was flown to England for medical treatment. She then went on to study at Oxford University and become a vocal advocate for human rights. Malala's story is an example of how someone can overcome adversity and emerge even stronger.

Both Sita and Malala faced difficult challenges, but they were able to overcome them through their resilience. They were both able to maintain hope and optimism in the face of adversity, and they were both able to find strength in their support systems. Their stories are an inspiration to us all, and they show us that it is possible to overcome even the most difficult challenges.

- **Diverse Leadership Styles**: Analyzing how different leadership styles can integrate aspects of Sita's resilience, whether it's through compassionate leadership, ethical governance, or transformative leadership.

  - **Transformative leadership:** Sita's unwavering faith in Rama and her ability to inspire hope and courage in others, even in the face of adversity, are qualities of a transformative leader. A modern-day example of a transformative leader who embodies these qualities is Nelson Mandela. Mandela spent 27 years in prison for his activism against apartheid in South Africa. During his imprisonment, he remained committed to his principles and refused to give up hope for a better future. When he was finally released from prison in 1990, he became the first black president of South Africa and worked to unite the country under a democratic government.

  - **Compassionate leadership:** Sita's deep empathy for others and her willingness to help those in need are qualities of a compassionate leader. A modern-day example of a compassionate leader who embodies these qualities is Mother Teresa. Mother Teresa dedicated her life to helping the poor and sick in Calcutta, India. She founded the Missionaries of Charity, a religious order that provides care for the dying, the lepers, and the orphans. Mother Teresa's work has inspired millions of people around the world to practice compassion and to help those in need.

- **Ethical governance:** Sita's unwavering commitment to truth and justice are qualities of an ethical leader. A modern-day example of an ethical leader who embodies these qualities is Mahatma Gandhi. Gandhi led the Indian independence movement against British rule using nonviolent civil disobedience. He believed that truth and justice would ultimately prevail, and he refused to compromise his principles, even in the face of violence and oppression. Gandhi's work has inspired millions of people around the world to fight for freedom and justice using peaceful means.

## Embracing Sita's Enduring Spirit

Sita's story in the Ramayana, far more than a historical or mythological account, is a beacon of resilience in the face of adversity. Her legacy teaches us to find inner strength, maintain our principles, and approach life's challenges with grace and dignity. For modern leaders and individuals alike, embracing these qualities can lead to a more compassionate, principled, and resilient approach to both personal and professional challenges. This chapter is not just a recounting of Sita's story; it's an invitation to weave her timeless wisdom into the fabric of our daily lives, allowing us to navigate our own journeys with the same fortitude and grace that defined hers.

# Chapter 5

# Lakshman:
# The Role of Loyalty and Support

In the multifaceted realm of modern leadership, where leaders grapple with complex decisions and ethical quandaries, the timeless narrative of the Ramayana provides invaluable insights, especially through the character of Lakshman. Esteemed not just as an ancient Indian epic, the Ramayana is a treasure trove of moral and philosophical wisdom. Among its rich array of characters, Lakshman stands out as a sterling example of unwavering loyalty and steadfast support. His dedication to his brother Rama, transcending personal desires and comforts, offers profound lessons for today's leaders in fostering an environment of trust, commitment, and collaborative strength.

---

### Fun Fact

According to some interpretations of the Ramayana, Lakshman never slept during the entire 14 years of exile in order to protect Rama and Sita. This dedication is commemorated in a ritual called "Lakshman Shakti," celebrated in parts of India, symbolizing the ultimate sacrifice and vigilance for the sake of duty.

This embodiment of loyalty and support by Lakshman can be seen as an essential tenet for leadership effectiveness in an era where transient loyalties and individualistic pursuits often overshadow collective goals. For leaders in contemporary settings, be it a corporate CEO navigating through market uncertainties or a community leader advocating for collective welfare, Lakshman's example serves as a beacon. His character exemplifies how steadfast support and unwavering loyalty can enhance leadership efficacy, build resilient teams, and facilitate the achievement of shared objectives.

The Ramayana, set in an age dominated by valiant heroes and profound sages, may seem distant from the modern-day corporate and social structures. Yet, the core principles it espouses, especially through Lakshman's life, are strikingly pertinent. His actions and choices underscore the importance of loyalty not as mere allegiance, but as a powerful force that strengthens leadership bonds, fosters team unity, and drives collective success.

In the vast epic of Ramayana, amidst the dazzling brilliance of Lord Rama, shines a quieter yet no less remarkable star: Lakshman. His unwavering loyalty and steadfast support form the bedrock upon which Rama's triumphs are built. But Lakshman's story transcends mere devotion; it offers practical lessons on being a loyal team member, a dependable partner, and a true brother-in-arms.

Lakshman's character in the Ramayana is a striking embodiment of unwavering loyalty and support. In an age where leadership is often challenged by fluctuating allegiances and self-interest, Lakshman's devotion to his brother Rama and his cause presents a compelling study in steadfast loyalty. His character offers invaluable lessons for contemporary leaders and team members, emphasizing the profound impact of steadfast support and fidelity in both personal and professional realms.

In today's complex leadership landscape, marked by rapid changes, diverse team dynamics, and ethical challenges, the ethos of loyalty and support as demonstrated by Lakshana is invaluable. His example inspires leaders to cultivate these virtues within their teams and organizations. By valuing and practicing unwavering support and loyalty, modern leaders can navigate their roles with a commitment that not only enhances team performance but also aligns with the broader values of trust, integrity, and collaborative success.

Fun Fact

Lakshman is also revered as the incarnation of Shesha, the serpent on which Vishnu rests. This connection symbolizes the depth of Lakshman's loyalty and his role as a foundation of support, reflecting the cosmic balance and eternal dedication found in Hindu mythology.

Thus, Lakshman's role in the Ramayana is not just a historical or mythological account but a resonant model for contemporary leadership. His unwavering dedication to Rama, transcending personal interests for the greater good, offers timeless lessons for today's leaders in building an ethos of loyalty and support within their realms of influence. This introduction sets the stage to explore how the virtues exemplified by Lakshman can be integrated into modern leadership practices, transforming the way leaders and teams interact, collaborate, and achieve their goals.

## Lakshman's Loyalty: A Pillar of Strength within the Ramayana's Ethos

In the grand narrative of the Ramayana, Lakshman stands out not just as a figure of valor but as a paragon of loyalty and unwavering support. His life's journey, deeply intertwined with that of his elder brother, Lord Rama, serves as a shining example of loyalty that transcends mere familial bonds, evolving into a profound testament of selfless commitment and solidarity.

Lakshman's devotion to Rama is characterized by a conscious and deliberate choice to stand by his brother, regardless of the challenges and sacrifices it entails. This choice, made at the outset of Rama's exile, marks a pivotal moment in Lakshman's life, where he forgoes the comforts and security of the palace to share in Rama's trials and tribulations. His decision to accompany Rama is driven not by obligation but by a deep-seated sense of duty, love, and respect.

Throughout the epic, Lakshman's actions reflect a loyalty that is dynamic and active. His decision to follow Rama into exile, and later, his unwavering support during the trials in the forest and the battle against Ravana, highlight his dedication to Rama's cause. Lakshman's loyalty is further exemplified in his interactions with Sita, where he showcases his commitment to protect and support her, even in the most challenging circumstances. This steadfast support goes beyond the call of duty, showcasing a loyalty born out of a deep understanding and shared vision with Rama.

Lakshman's life within the context of the Ramayana offers invaluable lessons for contemporary leaders and team members. His example illuminates the importance of loyalty as a dynamic and conscious choice, emphasizing the impact of steadfast support in achieving collective goals. In a world where loyalty is often challenged by external pressures and personal ambitions, Lakshman's devotion to Rama serves as a beacon, guiding individuals to prioritize the greater good and shared objectives over personal gains.

> **Fun Fact**
>
> There is a unique temple in India, Lakshman temple at Nalanda, Bihar, dedicated exclusively to Lakshman. This temple highlights his significance and the deep respect people have for his virtues of loyalty and devotion, which is less common as temples typically honor Rama or Hanuman from the Ramayana.

Thus, in the realms of both personal relationships and professional teamwork, Lakshman's loyalty within the Ramayana emerges as a timeless principle. It encourages individuals to cultivate a sense of commitment and support that is rooted in mutual respect, understanding, and a shared vision, transforming the dynamics of interpersonal relationships and collective endeavors. This chapter seeks to delve deeper into Lakshman's unwavering loyalty, exploring how this ancient virtue holds profound contemporary relevance and offers a framework for nurturing loyalty and support in various aspects of modern life.

> **Fun Fact**
>
> Did you know that the festival of Raksha Bandhan, celebrated in India, echoes the bond between Rama and Lakshman? Although primarily honoring the brother-sister relationship, the festival also symbolizes the protective nature of sibling bonds, reminiscent of Lakshman's unwavering support for Rama, reinforcing the societal value of loyalty and care within families and by extension, teams.

## Lakshman's Interactions and Loyalty Dynamics

Lakshman, a pivotal character in the Ramayana, exemplifies unwavering loyalty and supportive leadership, offering profound insights into team dynamics and interpersonal relationships in leadership roles. His interactions with key characters in the epic provide valuable lessons for modern leadership and team management.

1. **Supportive Role with Rama:    The Essence of Teamwork**

   Lakshman's relationship with Rama is the epitome of supportive teamwork. His decision to accompany Rama into exile was driven by deep loyalty and a sense of duty that transcends the obligations of brotherhood. This selfless act demonstrates the importance of solidarity in leadership and teamwork.

   - **Modern Implication:** In a corporate setting, a team member who shows unconditional support and commitment to their leader's vision, akin to Lakshman's support for Rama, is invaluable. This level of dedication fosters a strong, unified team capable of overcoming significant challenges.

   - **A real life example**

   - Sundar Pichai, the CEO of Google and Alphabet, and Ruth Porat, the company's Chief Financial Officer, exemplify the kind of supportive teamwork displayed by Rama and Lakshman. Their partnership, much like the brothers in the Ramayana, is characterized by unwavering loyalty, strategic counsel, and a shared commitment to the company's success.

   **Unconditional Support:**   When Pichai was appointed CEO in 2015, he faced the daunting task of leading a company going through significant internal changes. Porat, then the CFO, stood firmly by his side, publicly endorsing his vision and acting as a staunch advocate for his decisions. This unwavering support, similar to Lakshman's steadfast loyalty to Rama, provided Pichai with the confidence and stability needed to navigate the challenges of his new role.

**Strategic Counsel:** Porat's expertise in finance and business strategy has been instrumental in shaping Google's growth trajectory. She acts as a valuable sounding board for Pichai, offering insightful advice and challenging his assumptions when necessary. This dynamic mirrors Lakshman's role as Rama's strategic advisor, constantly offering alternative perspectives and ensuring well-rounded decision-making.

**Shared Vision:** Both Pichai and Porat are deeply invested in Google's long-term success. They share a clear vision for the company's future, focusing on innovation, technological advancement, and ethical responsibility. This alignment, reminiscent of Rama and Lakshman's unity of purpose, creates a cohesive leadership team that can effectively guide the company towards its goals.

The partnership between Pichai and Porat demonstrates how the principles of unwavering loyalty, strategic counsel, and shared vision, embodied by Lakshman in the Ramayana, remain relevant and impactful in the modern world. Their supportive teamwork serves as a model for leaders and team members alike, showcasing the power of collaboration and dedication in achieving organizational success.

2. **Protecting Sita:   The Role of Responsibility and Trust**

When Rama entrusts Sita's safety to Lakshman, it signifies a deep level of trust and responsibility. Lakshman's vigilant protection of Sita during Rama's absence highlights the importance of trust and reliability within a team.

- **Modern Implication:** In today's workplace, entrusting team members with critical responsibilities, as Rama did with Lakshman, can empower them and demonstrate confidence in their abilities. This trust can lead to increased accountability and a sense of ownership among team members.

- **A real life example**

- Satya Nadella, CEO of Microsoft, and Satya Gupta, EVP and president of Microsoft Cloud, offer a contemporary example of the trust-based responsibility demonstrated by Rama and Lakshman. When Nadella took over as CEO in 2014, he faced the challenge of revitalizing a company struggling to keep pace with changing technological trends. One of his key decisions was to empower Satya Gupta, a rising star within the company, with leading the development of Microsoft's cloud computing platform, Azure.

**Entrusted with Critical Responsibility:** Similar to Rama entrusting Sita's safety to Lakshman, Nadella placed his trust in Gupta's vision and abilities. He assigned Gupta the crucial task of spearheading Azure's growth, a responsibility that could significantly impact Microsoft's future. This act of trust demonstrated Nadella's confidence in Gupta's leadership and strategic mind, empowering him to make bold decisions and push boundaries.

**Accountability and Ownership:** Much like Lakshman's commitment to protecting Sita, Gupta embraced the responsibility entrusted to him with dedication and diligence. He led the Azure team with clear focus and passion, driving its growth into a market leader in cloud computing. This sense of ownership, fueled by Nadella's trust, fueled Gupta's team to innovate and achieve remarkable results.

**Shared Success:**   The success of Azure under Gupta's leadership has been instrumental in Microsoft's turnaround. The platform now generates a significant portion of the company's revenue and has positioned Microsoft as a major player in the cloud computing landscape. This shared success, akin to Rama and Lakshman's shared victory, highlights the power of trust and responsibility in unlocking potential and achieving collective goals.

The example of Nadella and Gupta illustrates how, even in a modern corporate setting, the timeless principles of Rama and Lakshman's story remain relevant. By nurturing trust and empowering team members with significant responsibility, leaders can unleash innovation, cultivate ownership, and drive collective success. This real-world parallel not only enhances the lesson's understanding but also emphasizes its applicability in diverse contexts, making the lessons learned universal and impactful.

3. **Interaction with Shabari:   Empathy and Respect**

Lakshman's interaction with Shabari, a devotee of Rama, reflects his humility and respect for all individuals, regardless of their social standing. This episode teaches the value of empathy and respect in leadership and teamwork.

- **Modern Implication:**   A leader or team member who respects and empathizes with colleagues from all levels of the organization, as Lakshman did with Shabari, creates an inclusive and respectful work environment. This approach enhances team morale and cooperation.

- **A real life example**

Jacinda Ardern, Prime Minister of New Zealand, and her response to the 2019 Christchurch mosque shootings offer a powerful example of the empathy and respect Lakshman displayed towards Shabari. In the face of an unimaginable tragedy, Ardern reached out to the Muslim community with genuine empathy and understanding, bridging the gap between political leadership and marginalized populations.

**Empathy and Humility**: Similar to Lakshmana's respectful interaction with Shabari, Ardern's response was characterized by deep empathy and humility. She visited grieving families personally, wore a headscarf as a sign of respect, and used her platform to amplify the voices of the Muslim community. This genuine display of empathy resonated deeply with people, creating a sense of unity and shared grief across New Zealand.

**Respect for All Individuals:**  Just as Lakshman treated Shabari with respect despite her humble background, Ardern ensured that all victims of the attack, regardless of their faith or origin, were treated with dignity and compassion. Her inclusive approach fostered national unity and countered attempts to stoke division in the aftermath of the tragedy.

**Leadership by Example:** Ardern's actions set a powerful example for leaders of all kinds. By demonstrating empathy and respect for all individuals, she fostered a more inclusive and compassionate society. This leadership style, reminiscent of Lakshman's treatment of Shabari, inspires others to bridge divides and promote understanding, fostering a stronger and more harmonious community.

The example of Jacinda Ardern and the Christchurch shooting response showcases how the leadership principles of empathy and respect, embodied by Lakshman in the Ramayana, remain crucial in the modern world. By applying these lessons to challenges of diversity, inclusion, and social justice, leaders can build stronger communities and navigate complex situations with grace and understanding. This real-world parallel further reinforces the universality of the lessons learned and their applicability in diverse contexts, making the takeaways more impactful and relevant to a wider audience.

4. **Relationship with Hanuman:   Collaboration and Mutual Respect**

Lakshman's interactions with Hanuman demonstrate mutual respect and collaboration. Their combined efforts in the search for Sita highlight the strength that lies in teamwork and collaborative problem-solving.

- **Modern Implication:**  Effective collaboration, as seen between Lakshman and Hanuman, is crucial in the modern workplace. When team members with diverse skills and perspectives work together respectfully, they can achieve exceptional outcomes.

- **A real life example**

The journey of SpaceX, aiming to revolutionize space exploration, exemplifies the collaborative teamwork demonstrated by Lakshman and Hanuman. At the helm are three individuals with distinct expertise and a shared, audacious vision: Elon Musk, the visionary leader; Gwynne Shotwell, the strategic operator; and Tom Mueller, the engineering mastermind. Their collaborative efforts, much like Lakshman and Hanuman's partnership, showcase the power of mutual respect and diverse skillsets in achieving seemingly impossible goals.

**Mutual Respect and Trust:** Despite their contrasting personalities and roles, a profound respect binds Musk, Shotwell, and Mueller. Musk recognizes Shotwell's sharp business acumen and trusts her to manage the company's financial and operational aspects. In turn, Shotwell admires Musk's ambition and readily translates his vision into concrete strategies. Similarly, Mueller's engineering genius is deeply valued by both, and his expertise shapes SpaceX's technological advancements. This mutual respect, akin to the bond between Lakshman and Hanuman, forms the bedrock of their successful collaboration.

**Diverse Skills, Unified Goal:** Just as Lakshman and Hanuman combined their strengths to serve Rama, Musk, Shotwell, and Mueller leverage their diverse talents to propel SpaceX forward. Musk's visionary leadership sets the direction, while Shotwell's business acumen ensures financial viability. Mueller's engineering prowess, meanwhile, translates ambition into reality, designing and building rockets that push the boundaries of space travel. This synergy of leadership, strategy, and execution mirrors the complementary skills of Lakshman and Hanuman, enabling them to overcome seemingly insurmountable challenges.

**Shared Success and Collaborative Spirit:** SpaceX's achievements, from reusable rockets to Starlink satellite internet, stand as a testament to the power of collaborative teamwork. Each milestone reached represents the combined efforts of a team that respects, trusts, and leverages each other's strengths. This collaborative spirit, reminiscent of Lakshman and Hanuman's unwavering support for Rama, has propelled SpaceX to the forefront of space exploration, inspiring the world with its audacity and innovation.

The example of SpaceX and its leadership team demonstrates how the principles of collaborative teamwork and mutual respect, embodied by Lakshman and Hanuman in the Ramayana, remain relevant and impactful in the modern world. By fostering an environment of trust, diversity, and shared goals, leaders can harness the collective power of their teams to achieve extraordinary outcomes, pushing the boundaries of innovation and leaving their mark on the world. This real-world parallel not only reinforces the lesson's value but also makes it relatable and applicable to contemporary audiences, ensuring the lessons resonate deeply and inspire action.

5. **Confrontation with Indrajit: Resilience and Perseverance**

   In his confrontation with Indrajit, Ravana's son, Lakshman exhibits remarkable resilience and perseverance. His ability to confront and overcome formidable challenges is a testament to his strength and dedication.

   - **Modern Implication:** Lakshman's resilience against Indrajit serves as a metaphor for overcoming business challenges. In the corporate world, resilience and perseverance are key qualities that help leaders and teams navigate through difficult times and emerge victorious.

- **A real life example**

The story of Lakshman's resilience in facing Indrajit finds a compelling echo in the journey of Mary Barra, CEO of General Motors (GM), and the company's remarkable turnaround after the 2008 financial crisis. Just as Lakshman persevered through injury and magical attacks to ultimately defeat Indrajit, Barra exhibited unwavering determination and strategic agility in navigating GM through bankruptcy, government bailouts, and a rapidly changing automotive landscape.

**Confronting a Formidable Challenge:** The 2008 financial crisis dealt a crippling blow to GM, pushing the iconic automaker to the brink of collapse. The company faced a mountain of debt, declining market share, and a workforce on the verge of despair. Much like Lakshmana facing the formidable Indrajit, Barra inherited a seemingly insurmountable challenge.

**Resilience and Strategic Innovation:** However, Barra, like Lakshman, refused to give up. She adopted a multi-pronged approach, focusing on cost-cutting, product innovation, and strategic partnerships. GM shed unprofitable brands, streamlined operations, and invested heavily in developing fuel-efficient and electric vehicles. This strategic agility, reminiscent of Lakshmana's tactical prowess against Indrajit, allowed GM to adapt to changing market demands and stay ahead of the competition.

**Emerging Victorious:**   After years of relentless effort, GM emerged from bankruptcy in 2009 a leaner, more agile company. Barra's leadership, marked by resilience and strategic foresight, had paid off. The company regained market share, launched successful new models like the Chevrolet Bolt electric car, and re-established itself as a leader in the automotive industry. This turnaround, akin to Lakshman's ultimate victory over Indrajit, stands as a testament to the power of perseverance and strategic thinking in the face of adversity.

By emulating the spirit of Lakshman and the leadership of Mary Barra, individuals and organizations can develop the resilience and strategic agility needed to overcome any obstacle and emerge victorious in the face of adversity. The timeless lessons from the Ramayana continue to resonate in the modern world, offering valuable guidance for navigating the complexities of business and achieving success.

## Interactive Elements for Deeper Engagement with Lakshman's Leadership Lessons

To facilitate a deeper understanding and personal application of the leadership lessons from Lakshman's character in the Ramayana, interactive elements can be incorporated into educational or training sessions. These elements aim to provoke introspection and self-assessment, allowing individuals to reflect on their own roles and behaviors in a team or leadership context, in light of the qualities exemplified by Lakshman.

### *Self-Reflection Questions*

1. **Examining Supportive Roles:**   Reflect on a situation where you played a supportive role in your team or organization. How

did you approach this role? Consider Lakshman's unwavering support for Rama. In what ways could you enhance your support to better align with Lakshman's example?

2. **Evaluating Loyalty in Difficult Times**:  Think of a challenging period in your professional life. How did you demonstrate loyalty to your team or organization? Were there moments where your loyalty was tested? Drawing inspiration from Lakshman's loyalty even in exile, how could you strengthen your commitment during tough times?

3. **Balancing Selflessness and Personal Goals**:  Contemplate a time when your personal goals conflicted with the needs of your team or organization. How did you handle this conflict? Assess how aligning with Lakshman's selfless dedication to a greater cause might have influenced your decisions and actions.

## *Leadership Assessment*

1. **Comparing Qualities with Lakshman**: Evaluate your own qualities as a team member or leader against those demonstrated by Lakshman, such as loyalty, support, resilience, and selflessness. Identify areas where you strongly align with these qualities and areas where you could improve.

2. **Identifying Areas for Growth**:  Based on your assessment, pinpoint specific areas for personal development. For instance, if you recognize a need to enhance your loyalty or support within a team, consider strategies to build these qualities, such as engaging in team-building activities or seeking feedback from peers and mentors.

3. **Action Plan for Development**:  Create a personalized action plan to cultivate the identified qualities. Set clear, achievable goals and outline steps to reach them. This could involve participating in leadership workshops, reading relevant

materials, or undertaking specific tasks within your team that allow you to practice and develop these qualities.

By engaging with these interactive elements, individuals can gain a deeper understanding of Lakshman's leadership qualities and how they can be applied in modern contexts. This process not only aids in learning but also encourages the practical application of these ancient principles in contemporary team dynamics and leadership scenarios, leading to personal growth and enhanced team effectiveness.

## Embracing Lakshman's Leadership Philosophy

Lakshman's loyalty and support in the Ramayana provide timeless insights into effective team dynamics and leadership. His interactions with various characters demonstrate the importance of trust, empathy, collaboration, and resilience in a team setting. By embracing Lakshman's leadership style, modern leaders and team members can foster more cohesive, supportive, and successful professional environments. This lesson is an invitation to integrate the qualities of Lakshman's character into contemporary leadership practices to enhance teamwork and achieve collective goals.

*Chapter 6*

# Hanuman:
# Unwavering Dedication and Service

In the dynamic landscape of contemporary leadership, where challenges are manifold and the call for ethical decision-making is ever-present, the ancient epic of the Ramayana emerges as a source of profound wisdom, particularly through the character of Hanuman. Revered not only as a pivotal figure in Indian mythology, Hanuman embodies the essence of unwavering dedication and selfless service, offering critical insights for leaders across various spheres today.

Hanuman's role in the Ramayana transcends the bounds of mere heroism; it epitomizes the pinnacle of devotion and commitment to a cause. In a world where shifting priorities and fleeting allegiances are commonplace, Hanuman's steadfastness and wholehearted dedication to Lord Rama present a compelling paradigm. His narrative is a powerful exemplar for modern leaders, whether they are steering corporations through turbulent markets or driving social change in their communities. Hanuman's unwavering focus and boundless energy underscore the potential of dedication and service in achieving extraordinary outcomes.

> **Fun Fact**
>
> In several villages across India, Hanuman is worshipped as a boundary guardian, often depicted in a fierce form standing at village borders to protect the inhabitants from evil spirits and negative influences. This role highlights his protective nature and the deep cultural roots of his worship.

Set against the backdrop of an era defined by mythological heroes and sagacious mentors, the Ramayana's teachings, as embodied by Hanuman, remain strikingly relevant. His deeds throughout the epic highlight the potency of dedication that is not blind zeal, but rather a conscious, purpose-driven commitment. Hanuman's journey, marked by formidable challenges and his unique ability to navigate them with agility, strength, and intelligence, is a masterclass in overcoming obstacles through sheer determination and loyalty.

> **Fun Fact**
>
> In addition to his might and wisdom, Hanuman is known for his mastery of music. Legend has it that he had a melodious voice and could sing the glories of Lord Rama in a way that could enchant anyone who listened. This aspect of his personality highlights the importance of art and culture in spiritual and devotional practices. Hanuman is also know have learned all the languages in the world in a day.

In the epic's vast tableau, Hanuman shines as a beacon of dynamic service and dedication. Beyond his supernatural feats, his character resonates deeply with contemporary themes of leadership: the ability to lead from the front, yet serve with humility; to possess immense power, yet exercise restraint; and to face insurmountable odds with unwavering optimism and creativity. His narrative provides invaluable lessons in resilience, adaptability, and the transformative power of devoted service.

> **Fun Fact**
>
> Hanuman is often depicted with a book or a pen, symbolizing his role as a scholar and a master of the scriptures. This representation is uncommon among deities known primarily for their physical strength, emphasizing that true power also lies in wisdom and knowledge.

Today's complex leadership scenarios, characterized by rapid technological advances, global challenges, and ethical complexities, call for the kind of dedicated leadership exemplified by Hanuman. His story inspires leaders to cultivate a sense of purpose that transcends personal ambitions, aligning with broader organizational or societal goals. It encourages a leadership style that harmonizes strength with empathy, authority with service, and ambition with humility.

> **Fun Fact**
>
> Hanuman is one of the few characters in Hindu mythology who is immortalized as Chiranjeevi, which means 'immortal' in Sanskrit. This status grants him the unique ability to live until the end of the current cosmic cycle, allowing him to protect and serve humanity throughout the ages.

Thus, Hanuman's portrayal in the Ramayana is not just an element of historical or mythological intrigue but a relevant, powerful exemplar for contemporary leadership. His extraordinary commitment and service to Rama, balancing power with purpose, offers timeless insights for today's leaders. This chapter aims to delve into how the qualities personified by Hanuman can be integrated into modern leadership practices, thereby enriching the way leaders approach their roles, foster team dynamics, and drive impactful outcomes in an ever-evolving world.

> **Fun Fact**
>
> One legend says that Hanuman, the monkey god, could leap all the way from India to Sri Lanka in a single bound – that's a distance of over 2,200 kilometers! That's like jumping from London to Moscow in one mighty leap! Talk about impressive wingspan!

## Hanuman's Unwavering Dedication and Service in the Ramayana

In the vibrant narrative of the Ramayana, Hanuman stands as a beacon of unwavering dedication and selfless service. His role, intricately connected to the saga of Lord Rama, showcases the profound impact of steadfast commitment and altruistic service, transcending the boundaries of personal interest and embodying a higher purpose.

Hanuman's relationship with Rama is a remarkable illustration of devotion that goes beyond conventional expectations. It is a choice deeply rooted in devotion, marked by an unparalleled sense of duty and an enduring allegiance. From his monumental leap to Lanka to his relentless quest for Sita, Hanuman's actions are driven by an unwavering commitment to Rama's cause, marked by a combination of strength, intelligence, and deep devotion.

> **Fun Fact**
>
> Hanuman's footprint is worshipped in a unique temple located in Sri Lanka, known as the 'Sri Pada' or the 'Sacred Footprint'. Devotees believe it to be the mark left by Hanuman when he was searching for Sita, making it a pilgrimage site that symbolizes his dedication and the impact of his journey across lands.

Throughout the Ramayana, Hanuman's contributions are characterized by proactive engagement and remarkable initiative.

His devotion is not passive; it actively shapes the course of events. His strength and wisdom, coupled with his humble approach and compassionate nature, create a multifaceted character who navigates challenges with a balanced blend of physical prowess and insightful acumen.

Hanuman's character in the Ramayana offers invaluable lessons for contemporary leadership and teamwork. His exemplary dedication highlights the importance of commitment to a cause and the transformative impact of selfless service. In a world where focus is often scattered, Hanuman's single-minded dedication to Rama's mission serves as an inspiration, emphasizing the power of unwavering commitment in achieving ambitious goals.

Fun Fact

In modern times, Hanuman's influence extends beyond spiritual realms into popular culture, with numerous comics, movies, and animated series being created about his adventures. These adaptations often highlight his virtues of courage, loyalty, and strength, making ancient wisdom accessible and inspirational to younger generations.

The narrative of Hanuman in the Ramayana transcends its mythological roots to become a timeless paradigm of dedication and service. It teaches that true commitment combines various qualities: strength, intelligence, humility, and a focused dedication to a cause. This chapter delves into Hanuman's profound dedication, exploring its relevance in today's world. It aims to draw lessons from his journey that resonate with contemporary challenges, inspiring individuals and teams to embody the essence of dedicated service in both their personal and professional endeavors.

# Hanuman: A Fiery Beacon of Service, Resourcefulness, and Unwavering Dedication

Hanuman, a central figure in the Ramayana, embodies unwavering dedication and selfless service, offering profound lessons in commitment and resilience. His role in the epic provides crucial insights for modern leadership and team dynamics, demonstrating the impact of steadfast dedication to a greater cause.

1. **Devotion to Rama:** Hanuman's unwavering devotion to Lord Rama in the Ramayana sets a gold standard for commitment and loyalty. His readiness to undertake perilous tasks, most notably his monumental leap to Lanka, is a prime example of his deep-seated dedication that transcends ordinary allegiance. Hanuman's actions were not just driven by duty; they were fueled by an intense devotion and a profound sense of purpose. His resolve to find Sita and deliver Rama's message, overcoming seemingly insurmountable obstacles, is a testament to his unparalleled commitment. This level of dedication, where personal risks and sacrifices are secondary to the accomplishment of the mission, highlights the importance of unwavering loyalty in achieving seemingly impossible feats.

   **Modern Implication:** In the contemporary professional world, Hanuman's type of dedication is a rare and invaluable asset. Team members who exhibit such deep commitment to their organization's vision and objectives become pivotal in driving success, especially in times of challenges and transitions. Their ability to stay focused on long-term goals, irrespective of immediate hurdles, fosters resilience and drives sustainable growth within organizations.

   **Leading with Hanuman's Unwavering Dedication:** In the corporate world, Tim Cook, the CEO of Apple Inc., embodies a similar level of commitment as seen in Hanuman's devotion to Rama. Succeeding Steve Jobs, a visionary leader with a unique legacy, Cook faced the daunting task of maintaining Apple's pioneering spirit and innovative edge. His leadership approach has been marked by a steadfast commitment to preserving the company's core values while navigating it through periods of significant technological and market changes. Cook's focus has been not just on sustaining Apple's success but also on furthering its legacy of innovation, ethical business practices, and customer-focused products. This alignment with the company's long-established vision, coupled with the courage to venture into new territories, echoes Hanuman's blend of dedication and adaptability. Cook's ability to balance respect for Apple's past with a vision for its future underlines the importance of unwavering dedication in leadership—a dedication that is as much about honoring the past as it is about building the future.

2.  **Hanuman's Ingenuity and Resourcefulness:** Hanuman's daring journey to Lanka in the Ramayana is a masterclass in ingenuity and resourcefulness. Faced with the daunting task of locating Sita in a hostile and unknown territory, Hanuman demonstrates remarkable adaptability and innovative thinking. His ability to change form, from minuscule to gigantic, to overcome physical barriers is a vivid example of his creative problem-solving skills. Moreover, his tactful interactions with adversaries and allies alike, coupled with his ability to assess situations and adapt his strategies accordingly, highlight the significance of agility and resourcefulness in overcoming challenging circumstances. Hanuman's journey is not just a physical

traversal but a journey of wit, intelligence, and adaptability, showcasing how creative solutions can turn obstacles into opportunities.

**Modern Implication:** In today's rapidly evolving business landscape, the ability to adapt and think creatively is crucial. Leaders and team members who exhibit these traits are invaluable in navigating complex and unpredictable challenges. The corporate world increasingly values individuals who can approach problems with a fresh perspective, think outside the box, and adapt their strategies to shifting circumstances. This agility in thought and action is essential for innovation, growth, and sustainability in any organization.

**Channelling Resourcefulness: Elon Musk's Innovative Leadership**

Elon Musk, CEO of Tesla and SpaceX, embodies Hanuman's spirit of resourcefulness and adaptability. Musk's approach to tackling complex engineering and business challenges draws parallels with Hanuman's journey to Lanka. Whether it's revolutionizing the automotive industry with electric cars at Tesla or conquering space travel barriers at SpaceX, Musk has consistently demonstrated an ability to think beyond conventional limits. His ventures are characterized by a willingness to take risks, a passion for innovation, and an unyielding drive to turn visionary ideas into reality.

Musk's journey, much like Hanuman's, involves navigating through uncharted territories. He faces challenges with a blend of creativity, strategic thinking, and tenacity. His ventures, though fraught with risks and uncertainties, are marked by breakthroughs that redefine industry standards. Musk's success in creating sustainable energy solutions and pursuing space exploration parallels Hanuman's success in his mission, underlining that with ingenuity and resilience, even the most ambitious goals can be achieved. This parallel between Hanuman's legendary resourcefulness and Musk's innovative leadership offers a compelling narrative on the power of creativity and adaptability in turning visionary ideas into tangible successes.

3. **Hanuman's Strength and Courage:** In the Ramayana, Hanuman's physical prowess and bravery are not merely about his supernatural abilities; they also signify his mental fortitude and readiness to face formidable challenges. His courage is most vividly illustrated in his confrontations during the battle in Lanka, where his fearlessness in the face of danger and his unwavering determination serve as a beacon of inspiration. Hanuman's strength lies not just in his physical capabilities but also in his mental resilience, his ability to remain undaunted in the face of adversity, and his commitment to his mission. This blend of physical and mental fortitude is a powerful testament to the essence of bravery, illustrating that true courage encompasses both resilience in adversity and the valor to confront challenges head-on.

**Modern Implication:** In today's dynamic business environment, leaders and team members face a myriad of challenges that require not just intellectual capabilities but also emotional strength. The ability to remain composed under pressure, to make decisive choices in the face of uncertainty, and to inspire confidence in others is paramount. Leaders who embody this blend of courage and resilience are instrumental in steering their organizations through turbulent times. Their fearless approach fosters a culture of confidence and resilience, encouraging teams to rise above challenges and perform at their best.

**Indra Nooyi's Fearless Leadership at PepsiCo**

Indra Nooyi, the former CEO of PepsiCo, exemplifies the fearless and resilient leadership akin to Hanuman's valor. During her tenure, Nooyi faced numerous challenges, from steering the company through economic downturns to making bold decisions about PepsiCo's product portfolio. Her approach to these challenges was marked by a unique blend of strategic foresight and courageous decision-making.

Nooyi's leadership involved transforming PepsiCo's product line to include healthier options, a move that was both daring and visionary. This decision, much like Hanuman's audacious endeavors, required stepping into uncharted territory and facing potential pushback. However, Nooyi's steadfastness and belief in her vision paved the way for PepsiCo's sustained growth and market leadership.

Her tenure at PepsiCo was also characterized by her ability to navigate complex market dynamics with agility and strength. Much like Hanuman's fearless approach in battle, Nooyi tackled business challenges with a bold and resilient mindset. Her leadership style not only strengthened PepsiCo's position in the global market but also inspired a generation of leaders. Nooyi's tenure at PepsiCo serves as a testament to the impact of courageous and resilient leadership in the corporate world, mirroring Hanuman's legacy of strength and valor in the face of daunting challenges.

4. **Hanuman's Compassion and Empathy:**  In the Ramayana, Hanuman's interaction with Sita in Lanka is a profound display of empathy and compassion. His meeting with Sita

is not just about conveying a message from Rama; it is a heartfelt connection where he fully grasps the depth of her distress. Hanuman's approach to Sita is marked by a deep understanding and sensitivity. He does not simply relay Rama's words but also offers solace and hope, showing a genuine concern for her wellbeing. This moment in the epic highlights the importance of emotional intelligence in communication. Hanuman's ability to empathize with Sita's situation, to listen and respond with care and understanding, is a testament to his emotional acuity. It showcases that effective communication, especially in times of distress, requires more than just words; it necessitates empathy, emotional connection, and the ability to provide reassurance and support.

**Modern Implication:** Emotional intelligence is a cornerstone of effective leadership and team management in the modern workplace. The capacity to recognize, understand, and respond to the emotional needs of team members is crucial in building trust, morale, and a supportive work environment. Leaders who are empathetic and attuned to the feelings of their team can foster better collaboration, enhance team dynamics, and create a workplace culture that values and supports its members. Empathy in leadership not only improves interpersonal relationships but also drives higher engagement and productivity.

**Sheryl Sandberg's Empathetic Leadership at Facebook**

Sheryl Sandberg, the Chief Operating Officer of Facebook, exemplifies empathetic leadership, mirroring the emotional intelligence shown by Hanuman. Known for her compassionate approach to leadership, Sandberg emphasizes the importance of understanding and addressing the emotional needs of her team. Her leadership style is characterized by active listening, open communication, and a genuine concern for the well-being of her colleagues.

Sandberg's approach to leadership became particularly impactful in the way she navigated personal tragedy - the loss of her husband - and how she shared her experience with vulnerability and openness. This not only humanized her as a leader but also resonated deeply with her team and the wider community, showcasing the strength that can be found in empathy and vulnerability.

At Facebook, Sandberg has fostered a culture that encourages support and understanding, much like Hanuman's empathetic approach with Sita. She advocates for creating an inclusive environment where employees feel valued and understood, reinforcing the belief that emotional intelligence is a vital component of successful leadership. Sandberg's leadership style demonstrates that empathy, compassion, and emotional connection are powerful tools in creating a positive and collaborative work environment, much like Hanuman's empathetic and compassionate interaction in the Ramayana.

5. **Hanuman's Selflessness and Sacrifice:** Hanuman's character in the Ramayana is a shining example of selflessness and dedication to a cause greater than oneself. His actions consistently demonstrate a willingness to put Lord Rama's mission above his personal needs and safety. This trait is vividly illustrated in his monumental leap to Lanka, where he faces immense risks not for personal glory but for the success of Rama's quest. Hanuman's selfless nature is not just about physical sacrifice; it also

encompasses his unwavering focus, his ability to put aside ego, and his commitment to the task at hand. His actions are driven by a deep sense of duty and devotion, making him an embodiment of selfless service.

**Modern Implication:** In the contemporary business world, selflessness and the ability to prioritize the organization's goals above personal accolades are invaluable qualities. Leaders who exhibit these traits can inspire collective effort and foster a team environment where the focus is on shared success rather than individual achievement. This approach is crucial for creating a unified team ethos, particularly in competitive and fast-paced business settings. Selflessness in leadership fosters collaboration, encourages mutual support, and aligns team members towards common objectives.

### Satya Nadella's Selfless Leadership at Microsoft

Satya Nadella, the CEO of Microsoft, exemplifies selfless leadership, echoing Hanuman's devotion to a greater purpose. Since taking the helm at Microsoft, Nadella has shifted the company's culture from one focused on individual achievements to one centered around collaboration and collective success. His leadership philosophy is rooted in the belief that the growth of the organization is intertwined with the growth of its people.

Nadella's focus on empathy, learning, and bringing people together has been instrumental in transforming Microsoft's work culture. He encourages his team to learn from failures and view them as opportunities for growth and innovation, a mindset that resonates with Hanuman's unyielding dedication to Rama's mission despite the challenges he faced. Under Nadella's guidance, Microsoft has not only seen a resurgence in its business success but has also cultivated an environment where employees feel valued and part of a larger purpose.

Nadella's approach demonstrates that leading with selflessness and a focus on collaborative success, much like Hanuman's dedication, is a powerful strategy in today's corporate landscape. It underscores the impact a leader can have in fostering a culture of teamwork, mutual respect, and shared aspirations, driving the organization towards collective achievement and sustainable growth.

## Interactive Elements for Deeper Engagement with Hanuman's Leadership Lessons

To deepen the understanding and personal application of leadership lessons derived from Hanuman's character in the Ramayana, incorporating interactive elements into educational or training sessions can be highly effective. These elements are designed to promote introspection and self-assessment, allowing individuals to reflect on their own roles and behaviors in a team or leadership context, in light of the qualities exemplified by Hanuman.

### *Self-Reflection Questions*

1. **Examining Dedication and Commitment:** Reflect on a scenario where your dedication was key to a project or team effort. How did you demonstrate commitment? In what ways can you incorporate Hanuman's level of dedication and focus to enhance your contribution in future projects?

2. **Resourcefulness in Problem-Solving:** Recall a challenging situation that required innovative problem-solving. How did you approach this challenge? Drawing inspiration from Hanuman's journey to Lanka, consider how you could employ

creativity and resourcefulness to overcome obstacles more effectively.

3. **Courage in Leadership:**  Think about a time when you faced a daunting challenge. How did you confront this situation? Reflect on how embodying Hanuman's bravery and strength could influence your approach to future challenges.

4. **Empathy and Emotional Intelligence:** Consider an instance where empathy played a role in your interactions with colleagues or team members. How did you display understanding and sensitivity? Assess how aligning more closely with Hanuman's empathetic approach could enhance your emotional intelligence and interpersonal relationships.

### *Leadership Assessment*

1. **Comparing Qualities with Hanuman:**  Evaluate your own qualities as a leader or team member against those shown by Hanuman, such as unwavering dedication, resourcefulness, bravery, and empathy. Identify areas where you resonate with these qualities and areas that require improvement.

2. **Identifying Areas for Growth:**  Based on your assessment, pinpoint specific areas where you can develop further. For instance, if you find room for improvement in displaying empathy or resourcefulness, consider strategies to strengthen these aspects, such as engaging in empathy-building activities or creative problem-solving exercises.

3. **Action Plan for Development:**  Formulate a personalized action plan to cultivate the identified qualities. Set specific, attainable goals and outline steps to achieve them. This could include participating in relevant workshops, reading materials that focus on these qualities, or taking on tasks within your

team that provide opportunities to practice and develop these skills.

Engaging with these interactive elements can help individuals gain a more profound understanding of Hanuman's leadership qualities and their application in contemporary settings. This introspective process encourages not only knowledge acquisition but also the practical application of these timeless principles, leading to personal growth and improved effectiveness in team and leadership roles.

## Embracing Hanuman's Leadership Philosophy

Hanuman's character in the Ramayana offers profound lessons in dedication, resourcefulness, courage, and empathy, each vital to effective leadership and team dynamics. His interactions and actions throughout the epic underscore the impact of these qualities in overcoming obstacles, inspiring trust, and achieving ambitious goals. Embracing Hanuman's leadership style, modern leaders and team members can cultivate a work environment that thrives on unwavering commitment, innovative thinking, bravery in the face of adversity, and a deep understanding of emotional dynamics.

His story is not just a narrative of mythological feats but a source of practical wisdom for today's leadership challenges. Hanuman's journey, marked by his devotion to Rama and his ability to surmount daunting challenges creatively and bravely, sets a benchmark for leadership excellence. His empathy, particularly in his interactions with Sita, exemplifies emotional intelligence, a crucial component in today's leadership landscape where understanding and addressing the emotional needs of team members is key to building a supportive and effective work culture.

By adopting Hanuman's qualities, leaders and teams can navigate the complexities of the modern professional world with a renewed sense of purpose, creativity, and emotional awareness. This lesson is more than a study of a legendary figure; it is a call to action for incorporating these age-old virtues into contemporary leadership models. Integrating Hanuman's character traits into daily practices can significantly enhance teamwork, foster innovation, and lead to the achievement of collective goals.

Hanuman's example in the Ramayana is a beacon for contemporary leadership, offering timeless wisdom that is as relevant today as it was in the ancient world. His story encourages leaders and teams to strive for excellence, not just through skill and intellect but also through heart and commitment, truly embodying the spirit of dedication and service.

# Chapter 7

# The Power of Choices: Lessons from Bharata and Vibhishana

In the intricate fabric of leadership and decision-making that defines our contemporary world, the ancient saga of the Ramayana emerges not just as a mythological narrative but as a repository of profound wisdom, particularly exemplified by characters like Bharata and Vibhishana. Their stories, deeply woven into the telling of this epic, provide illuminating insights into the power of choices and their far-reaching consequences.

The narratives of Bharata and Vibhishana stand out for their emphasis on the ethical and moral crossroads faced by leaders. In a time where decisions often hold the weight of unforeseen outcomes, their choices in the Ramayana serve as compelling case studies. Bharata, despite being offered the throne, chooses to remain loyal to the principles of righteousness and his brother Rama's rightful claim to the throne. Vibhishana, on the other hand, makes the bold decision to leave his brother Ravana and align with Rama, driven by his commitment to dharma (righteous duty) over familial ties.

The divergent paths taken by Bharata and Vibhishana highlight the complex interplay of duty, morality, and loyalty in leadership. Their decisions, set against the rich backdrop of an epic battle between good and evil, underscore the enduring relevance of ethical decision-making in today's leadership landscape. Whether it's navigating corporate strategies or steering social initiatives, the choices made by leaders can have a transformative impact on their organizations and the wider community.

In an era marked by rapid change and ethical ambiguities, the decisions made by Bharata and Vibhishana resonate with significant implications. Bharata's refusal to usurp the throne in favor of upholding his brother's right and Vibhishana's alignment with virtue over familial loyalty offer profound lessons in prioritizing ethical integrity over personal gain. These choices demonstrate the courage and foresight required to navigate the complex moral landscapes of contemporary leadership.

This chapter will explore the depths of Bharata and Vibhishana's choices within the Ramayana's grand narrative. It aims to unravel how their decisions, driven by a deep sense of duty and ethical clarity, provide invaluable lessons for modern leaders. By examining their stories, we can glean insights into making choices that not only serve immediate goals but also align with higher principles of integrity and righteousness, thereby shaping a legacy that stands the test of time.

Through the lens of Bharata and Vibhishana's experiences, this lesson seeks to offer guidance to today's leaders on making impactful decisions. It underscores the significance of choosing paths that harmonize personal ambitions with ethical responsibilities, thereby fostering leadership that is both effective and morally sound in our complex and dynamic world.

## Bharata: The Epitome of Selfless Leadership and Ethical Governance

In the ancient epic of the Ramayana, Bharata stands as a remarkable figure, exemplifying the virtues of selfless leadership and unwavering commitment to ethical governance. His character, often overshadowed by the heroics of his brother Lord Rama, provides critical lessons in principled leadership, resonating strongly with the complexities of today's leadership challenges. Bharata's journey is a compelling narrative of integrity, selflessness, and devotion to duty, underscoring these traits as essential for respected and effective leadership.

When presented with the kingship of Ayodhya, Bharata's refusal to ascend the throne in place of his exiled brother Rama is a profound demonstration of his moral integrity. Choosing to honor his father's word and Rama's right to the throne, Bharata makes a decision that defies personal ambition and underscores his adherence to dharma (righteous duty). Governing the kingdom as a steward rather than as a sovereign, he places Rama's sandals on the throne, symbolizing his commitment to uphold his brother's rightful rule. This poignant act is not only an embodiment of humility but also a powerful testament to Bharata's dedication to righteous leadership and the well-being of his people.

Bharata's role as a ruler is characterized by fairness, justice, and an unwavering dedication to the welfare of his subjects. He leads not for personal glory but with a sense of duty to the kingdom, ensuring his governance aligns with the highest ethical and moral standards. This selfless approach to leadership, prioritizing the common good above personal gain, is a vital lesson for contemporary leaders. It highlights the significance of ethical decision-making and integrity in fostering trust and loyalty among stakeholders.

In addition, Bharata's leadership style is marked by inclusivity and collaborative decision-making. He values the counsel of his advisors, actively involving them in the governance process. This approach of empowering others and embracing diverse viewpoints is highly relevant in modern organizational contexts. It promotes a participatory and inclusive culture where team members feel valued and are encouraged to contribute their unique perspectives, leading to more holistic and effective outcomes.

Bharata's narrative in the Ramayana, therefore, is not just a historical or mythological account, but a relevant blueprint for contemporary leadership. His qualities of selflessness, ethical governance, and commitment to duty offer invaluable insights for today's leaders. By embodying these virtues, leaders can cultivate a culture of trust, respect, and long-term success, ensuring their leadership not only achieves immediate goals but also contributes to a lasting positive legacy.

**Bharata's Ethical Choice and Selfless Governance**: In the Ramayana, Bharata is faced with a profound moral dilemma when he is offered the throne of Ayodhya in the absence of his brother, Lord Rama. His decision to refuse the throne and instead govern the kingdom in Rama's name, using Rama's sandals as a symbol of his rightful rule, is a powerful testament to his ethical principles and selfless nature. Bharata's choice highlights the essence of true leadership, which places duty and righteousness above personal ambition and gain.

**Modern Implication**: In the modern business world, leaders often encounter situations that test their ethical boundaries and personal ambitions. Bharata's example serves as a guiding light, advocating for leadership that prioritizes ethical decision-making and the welfare of stakeholders over personal gain. Leaders who embrace this approach not only foster trust and loyalty among their team members but also establish a legacy of integrity and moral governance.

**Paul Polman's Ethical Leadership at Unilever:**   Paul Polman, former CEO of Unilever, stands out as a modern exemplar of ethical leadership, much like Bharata in the Ramayana. Upon taking the helm of Unilever in 2009, Polman was faced with the challenge of driving growth in a competitive global market while also addressing environmental and social sustainability issues. He made a bold decision to redefine the company's strategy, focusing not solely on short-term profits but on long-term sustainability and ethical practices.

Polman introduced the Unilever Sustainable Living Plan, aiming to decouple the company's growth from its environmental footprint, while increasing its positive social impact. This plan set ambitious targets, including sourcing 100% of agricultural raw materials sustainably and enhancing the health and well-being of over a billion people.

In a move reminiscent of Bharata's refusal of the throne, Polman famously stopped quarterly reporting to shareholders, a practice dominated by short-term financial metrics. He argued that this short-termism was inconsistent with the long-term sustainability goals he envisioned for Unilever. This decision was risky, as it could have led to a backlash from shareholders focused on immediate returns, but it underscored his commitment to ethical governance and long-term value creation.

Polman's leadership dramatically transformed Unilever. The company not only saw an increase in its share price but also became a global leader in sustainability. Under his tenure, Unilever was regularly recognized for its leadership in corporate sustainability indices. Polman's approach fostered trust and loyalty among stakeholders, from employees to consumers, who saw Unilever as a company genuinely committed to doing good.

Polman's tenure at Unilever offers a compelling real-life parallel to Bharata's ethical and selfless governance in the Ramayana. His decision to prioritize long-term sustainability over short-term profits, much like Bharata's decision to rule in Rama's stead, highlights the impact of ethical leadership in the modern business world. Polman's legacy at Unilever is a testament to the fact that ethical decision-making and a commitment to the greater good can lead to both business success and a positive societal impact.

**Bharata's Devotion to Duty and Team Empowerment:**  Bharata's reign in Ayodhya, serving as a caretaker until Rama's return, is marked by his devotion to duty and his efforts to empower his team. He leads not as a monarch, but as a steward of Rama's principles, ensuring that the kingdom thrives in the true spirit of its rightful ruler. This approach underscores the importance of empowering team members and leading by example, fostering a culture of shared values and collective responsibility.

**Modern Application:**  In contemporary leadership, this translates into empowering employees, decentralizing decision-making, and creating an organizational culture that reflects shared values and objectives. Leaders who empower their teams to take ownership and make decisions in line with the organization's core values promote a sense of collective responsibility and shared success.

**Howard Schultz's Leadership at Starbucks:**  Howard Schultz, the CEO of Starbucks, is a modern example of a leader who embodies Bharata's devotion to duty and team empowerment. When Schultz returned as CEO in 2008, Starbucks was facing a challenging period. He recognized that the way forward was not just through strategic changes but also by empowering his employees, whom he famously refers to as "partners".

Schultz's approach was to create a culture where every employee felt a sense of ownership and responsibility towards the company. He introduced comprehensive training programs, provided employees with stock options, and involved them in decision-making processes. This strategy was akin to Bharata's style of governance, where he empowered his team and led by upholding Rama's values.

Under Schultz's leadership, Starbucks held open forums where employees at all levels were encouraged to voice their opinions and ideas. This open communication policy ensured that the employees felt heard and valued, similar to how Bharata would have listened to and valued the input of his advisors and subjects.

Schultz's leadership focused on aligning the company's operations with its core values, such as ethical sourcing, environmental stewardship, and community engagement. He ensured that Starbucks' growth strategies were in harmony with these values, thereby creating a sense of shared purpose among the employees.

The result of Schultz's leadership was a revitalized Starbucks that not only recovered from its downturn but also grew to new heights. The company saw increased employee satisfaction, customer loyalty, and financial success. Schultz's approach to empowering his team and leading with a commitment to shared values and objectives mirrors Bharata's principled stewardship in Ayodhya.

Howard Schultz's tenure at Starbucks exemplifies how a leader's devotion to duty and focus on team empowerment can transform an organization. Like Bharata, Schultz led with a sense of stewardship, empowering his "partners" and aligning the company's growth with its core values. His leadership style demonstrates the effectiveness of empowering employees and fostering a culture of shared responsibility, which can lead to sustainable success and a positive organizational legacy.

## Vibhishana: A Paradigm of Ethical Choices and Principled Alliance in the Ramayana

In the epic saga of the Ramayana, Vibhishana emerges as a character of profound ethical complexity and principled decision-making. His narrative offers deep insights into the challenges of ethical leadership, particularly in the face of conflicting loyalties and moral dilemmas. As the brother of Ravana, the king of Lanka and the antagonist in the epic, Vibhishana's decision to align with Lord Rama – an enemy of his own kingdom – is a striking illustration of choosing righteousness over familial and national allegiance. This choice, steeped in moral and ethical considerations, makes Vibhishana a compelling figure for contemporary leaders grappling with complex ethical decisions.

Vibhishana's journey is emblematic of the struggle between personal loyalty and universal dharma (righteous duty). Despite his ties to Ravana and Lanka, he is deeply troubled by Ravana's unethical actions, particularly the abduction of Sita. Vibhishana's decision to leave Lanka and seek refuge with Rama is a testament to his commitment to dharma, prioritizing ethical principles over personal relationships and power. His choice underscores the importance of adhering to one's moral compass, even when it means making difficult decisions that may go against personal or societal expectations.

As an advisor to Rama, Vibhishana's role is pivotal in the epic battle against Ravana. His insights into Lanka's strengths and weaknesses and his strategic counsel are invaluable, highlighting the role of integrity and knowledge in leadership. Vibhishana's contributions to Rama's victory exemplify how ethical choices can lead to meaningful collaborations and positive outcomes. His alliance with Rama, based on shared values and mutual respect, offers a powerful example of principled collaboration in pursuit of a common good.

In the modern context, Vibhishana's story resonates with leaders facing ethical quandaries, where making the right choice often involves difficult trade-offs. His narrative encourages leaders to weigh their decisions against ethical standards and to have the courage to stand by their convictions, even in the face of adversity or unpopular opinion. It also illustrates the value of principled alliances and the strength that can be derived from collaborations built on a foundation of mutual trust and ethical congruence.

Thus, Vibhishana's portrayal in the Ramayana is not merely a tale from antiquity but a relevant and instructive example for contemporary leadership. His story offers profound insights into the dynamics of ethical decision-making, the courage to choose righteousness, and the power of alliances grounded in moral principles. It challenges today's leaders to reflect on their choices and to lead in a manner that aligns with the deeper values of integrity, justice, and ethical responsibility.

## Vibhishana's Principled Stance and Strategic Alliance: Lessons in Ethical Decision-Making and Collaborative Success

Vibhishana exemplifies the profound impact of making ethical decisions and forming strategic alliances based on principled values. His story offers valuable insights into the complexities of leadership, especially when facing moral dilemmas and choosing alliances.

Faced with the moral quandary of opposing his brother Ravana, the king of Lanka, Vibhishana makes a pivotal decision that defines his character. His choice to leave Lanka and ally with Lord Rama, despite being perceived as betrayal by his own kingdom, is driven by a deep sense of dharma (righteous duty) and a commitment to ethical principles. Vibhishana's decision to support Rama, who stands for justice and moral righteousness, over Ravana, who had strayed from the path of dharma, underscores the significance of aligning with values and ethics over personal ties and immediate benefits. This act of choosing what is right over what is convenient or advantageous is a powerful message for leaders today, emphasizing the importance of ethical decision-making in leadership.

Vibhishana's role in Rama's victory in Lanka is not just a testament to his loyalty but also to his strategic acumen. His intimate knowledge of Lanka and his advice play a crucial role in Rama's success, illustrating the value of strategic alliances formed on the basis of shared principles and mutual respect. Vibhishana's alliance with Rama is a collaboration that brings together complementary strengths and capabilities, benefiting both parties and leading to a shared victory. This aspect of Vibhishana's story highlights the effectiveness of forming alliances that are not just based on mutual interests but are also grounded in shared ethical values and objectives.

**Modern Implication:** In the contemporary business landscape, leaders often face the challenge of choosing partners and forming alliances. Vibhishana's story serves as a guiding principle, advocating for collaborations that are rooted in shared values and ethical congruence. Leaders who form partnerships based on mutual respect, shared goals, and a commitment to ethical practices can achieve greater success and long-term sustainability.

Such alliances are built on a solid foundation of trust and integrity, leading to more robust and enduring partnerships.

**Satya Nadella's Collaborative Success at Microsoft:** Satya Nadella, CEO of Microsoft, exemplifies the kind of strategic and principled alliance-building seen in Vibhishana's story. Since taking over as CEO in 2014, Nadella has focused on transforming Microsoft's culture and strategic partnerships, emphasizing collaboration, innovation, and ethical practices. One of Nadella's significant moves was shifting Microsoft's approach from being competitive to being more collaborative, both internally and with external partners.

Nadella's decision to collaborate with companies that were once considered rivals, such as Apple and Linux, was a strategic move that mirrored Vibhishana's alliance with Rama. These partnerships were based on the recognition of mutual strengths and the potential for shared success. Under Nadella's leadership, Microsoft has not only enhanced its product offerings but also improved its market position and brand image.

Furthermore, Nadella's focus on ethical technology, responsible AI, and sustainability aligns with the ethical underpinnings of Vibhishana's choices. By prioritizing ethical considerations in its partnerships and business practices, Microsoft under Nadella has established itself as a leader in responsible and sustainable technology.

Nadella's leadership at Microsoft demonstrates how strategic alliances, when built on a foundation of shared values and mutual respect, can lead to transformative outcomes. His approach mirrors the lessons from Vibhishana's story in the Ramayana, highlighting the importance of ethical decision-making and collaborative success in contemporary leadership.

## Vibhishana's Wisdom and Counsel: Navigating Ethical Dilemmas in Leadership

Vibhishana is renowned for his wisdom and insightful counsel, characteristics that are crucial in the realm of modern leadership. His role in the narrative not only demonstrates the importance of sound judgment but also highlights how ethical counsel can profoundly influence the course of events.

In the Ramayana, Vibhishana's decision to leave his brother Ravana and join Rama, despite the potential accusations of betrayal, stems from his deep moral convictions and understanding of dharma (righteousness). His counsel to Rama during the battle is not only strategic but also ethically grounded, reflecting his wisdom and deep understanding of the complexities of the situation. This act of providing counsel that balances practicality with ethical considerations illustrates the importance of wisdom in leadership - making decisions that are not only effective but also morally sound.

**Modern Leadership Implications:** Vibhishana's example is exceedingly relevant in today's leadership context, where decision-makers are frequently confronted with complex situations that require both strategic acumen and moral insight. The ability to provide counsel that is both wise and ethically informed is a valuable trait in leaders across various fields. It involves understanding the broader impact of decisions, considering the well-being of all stakeholders, and upholding ethical standards, even in challenging situations.

Leaders today can learn from Vibhishana's example to cultivate a leadership style that is reflective, informed, and morally grounded. This approach not only aids in navigating through complex scenarios but also builds trust and respect among team members and stakeholders.

**Ruth Bader Ginsburg's Judicial Wisdom:**   A modern embodiment of the type of wisdom and counsel exemplified by Vibhishana can be seen in the late Justice Ruth Bader Ginsburg of the U.S. Supreme Court. Known for her sharp intellect and principled stand on various issues, Ginsburg's judicial decisions and opinions were marked by a deep understanding of the law, societal implications, and ethical considerations. Her counsel on critical legal matters, much like Vibhishana's advice to Rama, was not just legally sound but also underscored by a strong moral compass, influencing significant rulings that shaped the social and legal landscape.

Ginsburg's legacy as a jurist and a leader highlights the impact of wisdom and ethical counsel in making decisions that have far-reaching consequences. Her ability to balance legal acumen with ethical reasoning serves as a powerful example for leaders in all sectors, illustrating how informed and principled guidance can lead to just and effective outcomes.

To incorporate the qualities of Vibhishana's wisdom and counsel into modern leadership practices, training programs can focus on developing leaders' ability to think critically, understand ethical implications, and provide balanced guidance. This involves cultivating a deep understanding of one's field, staying informed about broader societal issues, and developing a strong ethical framework to guide decision-making.

By embracing Vibhishana's approach to wisdom and counsel, leaders can navigate the complexities of the modern world with a balanced perspective, making decisions that are not only effective but also uphold the highest ethical standards.

# Embracing Ethical Leadership: The Enduring Legacies of Bharata and Vibhishana

The narratives of Bharata and Vibhishana in the Ramayana offer profound lessons for contemporary leadership, emphasizing the pivotal role of ethics, integrity, and wise counsel in navigating the complexities of decision-making. Their stories transcend the bounds of an ancient epic, providing timeless insights into the essence of moral governance and principled leadership.

**Bharata's Legacy of Ethical Governance:**   Bharata's refusal to usurp the throne and his decision to rule Ayodhya as a steward of Rama's principles exemplify a leadership approach grounded in selflessness and ethical integrity. His commitment to duty over personal gain sets a high standard for modern leaders. It illustrates that true leadership is not about holding power but about serving with a sense of responsibility and righteousness. Bharata's actions remind us that ethical governance, characterized by respect for rightful authority and dedication to the welfare of all, fosters trust, loyalty, and long-term success.

**Vibhishana's Emblem of Wise Counsel:** Vibhishana's role, marked by his insightful counsel and commitment to dharma, highlights the importance of wisdom in leadership. His ability to provide balanced, ethical advice in the midst of conflict underscores the value of counsel that harmonizes strategic thinking with moral principles. Vibhishana teaches us that leaders must be not only strategic thinkers but also ethical guides, capable of influencing positive outcomes through sound judgment and integrity.

**Synthesizing Their Teachings in Modern Leadership:** The stories of Bharata and Vibhishana serve as beacons for leaders in various spheres – from corporate boardrooms to social enterprises. They exemplify how ethical considerations and wise counsel are fundamental to effective leadership. By integrating the principles exemplified by these characters, modern leaders can navigate the challenges of their roles more effectively and ethically.

Leaders can draw inspiration from Bharata's selflessness and commitment to duty, ensuring that their decisions prioritize the collective good over personal ambition. Similarly, they can learn from Vibhishana's wisdom and ability to provide counsel that is both pragmatic and ethically sound, fostering decision-making processes that are inclusive, balanced, and morally responsible.

The lessons from Bharata and Vibhishana's lives in the Ramayana are not mere historical or mythological anecdotes; they are relevant, powerful guides for contemporary leadership. Their legacies teach us that ethical leadership and wise counsel are not just idealistic concepts but practical, essential qualities that can lead to sustainable success and respect. By embracing these values, today's leaders can navigate their roles with a sense of moral responsibility, integrity, and wisdom, thereby making a meaningful impact in their organizations and society at large.

# Chapter 8

# Overcoming Obstacles: Insights from the Bridge to Lanka

In the timeless narrative of the Ramayana, the episode of building the bridge to Lanka stands as a remarkable allegory of overcoming obstacles, embodying a wealth of wisdom for contemporary leaders and decision-makers. This historic endeavor, more than just an architectural marvel, serves as an inspiring metaphor, illustrating how unity, innovation, and unwavering determination can triumph over the most daunting challenges.

The saga of Rama's army, comprised of diverse beings, coming together to construct a bridge across the ocean to rescue Sita, is a powerful testament to collaborative effort, strategic problem-solving, and perseverance. The construction of this bridge, under Rama's leadership, is not merely a physical conquest but a journey that encapsulates the essence of overcoming barriers through collective endeavor and shared vision.

In our modern world, characterized by rapid changes and complex challenges, the story of the bridge to Lanka provides profound insights into the art of navigating difficulties. It symbolizes the potential of cohesive teamwork in overcoming seemingly insurmountable hurdles, highlighting the importance of each individual's contribution towards achieving a common goal. The bridge represents not just a physical pathway but a journey of resilience, innovation, and shared aspirations.

Leaders and teams today can draw significant lessons from this epic event. The collaborative spirit of Rama's army, the strategic ingenuity in constructing the bridge, and the unwavering focus on the mission resonate deeply with the requirements of contemporary leadership. Whether it's steering a company through a turbulent market or leading a community initiative, the principles exemplified in this endeavor are universally applicable and immensely instructive.

This chapter delves into the multifaceted lessons gleaned from the construction of the bridge to Lanka. It aims to explore how the principles of teamwork, innovation, and perseverance, as demonstrated in this legendary undertaking, can be applied in modern contexts. By dissecting the strategies employed and the dynamics of collaboration in this monumental task, we aim to uncover the essence of overcoming obstacles, not only in physical terms but also in the realms of leadership, strategy, and personal growth.

The journey to build the bridge to Lanka, fraught with challenges yet triumphant in its conclusion, serves as a beacon for leaders and teams navigating the complex landscapes of the modern world. It offers a blueprint for converting adversities into opportunities, highlighting how collective strength, strategic foresight, and steadfast commitment can pave the way for remarkable achievements.

In a world where obstacles often seem insurmountable, the story of the bridge to Lanka stands as a testament to the power of human spirit and collaboration. This chapter seeks to unravel the timeless wisdom embedded in this epic tale, offering contemporary leaders and teams insights into mastering the art of overcoming obstacles with grace, ingenuity, and collective effort.

## Overcoming Obstacles: Insights from the Bridge to Lanka

### 1. Harnessing Collective Strength and Unity

**Lesson from the Ramayana:** In the Ramayana, the construction of the bridge to Lanka is a remarkable example of harnessing collective strength and unity. This monumental task was accomplished not by a single entity but through the collaborative efforts of diverse groups. The vanara (monkey) army, along with various mythical creatures, each contributed their unique abilities and resources. The vanaras, known for their extraordinary strength and agility, worked alongside others, each playing a crucial role. This episode illustrates how pooling diverse skills and strengths can overcome even the most daunting challenges. The unity and teamwork displayed in building the bridge symbolize the power of collective effort, where the sum is greater than its parts.

**Modern Application:** In the contemporary world of business and organizational management, this lesson translates into the value of embracing diversity and fostering teamwork. In an organization, each member brings unique skills, experiences, and perspectives. By recognizing and harnessing these diverse talents, a team can achieve much more than any individual working alone. This approach requires leaders to create an environment where collaboration is encouraged, and different viewpoints are valued. It involves breaking down silos, encouraging cross-functional teams, and cultivating a culture where innovative ideas can emerge from the synergy of diverse contributions. This strategy not only leads to innovative solutions but also builds a more inclusive and dynamic work environment.

**NASA's International Space Station:** The construction and operation of the International Space Station (ISS) epitomize the essence of this lesson. The ISS project, one of the most ambitious international collaborations in human history, brought together space agencies from the USA (NASA), Russia (Roscosmos), Europe (ESA), Japan (JAXA), and Canada (CSA). Despite the complexities of coordinating across different languages, cultural backgrounds, technical standards, and political landscapes, the ISS has been a testament to what can be achieved through international cooperation. Each agency contributed its unique expertise and resources - from technology and spacecraft to human resources and research capabilities. The ISS serves as a scientific laboratory, a symbol of diplomatic cooperation, and a beacon of human ingenuity, made possible by the collective strength and unity of multiple nations. It demonstrates how collaborative efforts can transcend individual capabilities, leading to groundbreaking achievements and advancements for humanity.

## 2. Strategic Innovation and Problem-Solving

**Lesson from the Ramayana:** The construction of the bridge to Lanka in the Ramayana is an outstanding example of strategic innovation and problem-solving. The narrative highlights that the successful completion of the bridge was not merely a result of physical labor or brute force but a triumph of ingenious thinking and adaptability. The idea to use floating stones, a concept that defied conventional engineering wisdom, symbolizes the power of innovative solutions in overcoming obstacles. This approach required not just physical resources but also a creative mindset, a willingness to experiment, and the ability to adapt strategies in response to unique challenges. The construction of the bridge, therefore, is a metaphor for the importance of thinking beyond traditional methods and embracing innovative solutions to solve complex problems.

**Modern Application:** In today's fast-paced business environment, strategic innovation is crucial in navigating challenges and staying ahead of the competition. Leaders must cultivate an organizational culture that encourages creative thinking and is open to exploring unconventional ideas. This involves creating a safe space for experimentation, where failure is seen as a stepping stone to innovation rather than a setback. It also means investing in research and development, encouraging cross-functional collaborations, and staying attuned to emerging trends and technologies. By fostering an environment where out-of-the-box thinking is celebrated and new ideas are actively pursued, organizations can unlock groundbreaking innovations and turn challenges into opportunities for growth and transformation.

**Apple and iPhone:**  Apple Inc.'s introduction of the iPhone is a perfect illustration of strategic innovation in the face of challenges. At a time when the mobile phone market was saturated with traditional designs and functionalities, Apple dared to think differently. The iPhone, with its user-friendly interface, touch screen, and integration of phone, internet, and multimedia capabilities, was not just a new product; it was a redefinition of what a mobile phone could be. Apple's innovative approach transformed the smartphone industry, setting new benchmarks for technology, design, and functionality. This success was a result of Apple's commitment to innovation, its willingness to break away from the norm, and its vision of creating products that redefine market standards. The iPhone's impact on the technology industry and consumer habits worldwide echoes the Ramayana's lesson on the power of strategic innovation and creative problem-solving in overcoming obstacles and achieving remarkable success.

## 3.  Persistence and Perseverance

**Lesson from the Ramayana:**  The arduous task of building the bridge to Lanka in the Ramayana is a profound testament to the virtues of persistence and perseverance. The narrative illustrates how Rama and his army faced a multitude of challenges, including daunting natural obstacles, logistical constraints, and time pressures. Despite these hurdles, they exhibited unwavering determination and relentless effort. Their persistence was driven by a strong purpose and an unshakeable belief in their mission. This part of the Ramayana encapsulates the essence of perseverance - the ability to stay the course despite facing setbacks and to maintain focus and dedication towards achieving a goal. It underscores the message that steadfastness and relentless effort are crucial in turning visions into reality.

**Modern Application:**  In the realm of contemporary leadership and business, persistence and perseverance are indispensable qualities for success. Leaders are often confronted with complex challenges, unexpected setbacks, and even failures. The key to navigating these obstacles lies in fostering a culture of resilience and steadfast determination. It is essential for leaders to inspire their teams to stay committed to their goals, to learn from setbacks, and to view challenges as opportunities for growth and innovation. Encouraging a mindset of perseverance helps build a resilient team that can adapt to changes and persist in the face of adversity. Moreover, leaders themselves must lead by example, demonstrating tenacity and resilience, thereby motivating their teams to embrace these qualities.

**SpaceX:**  SpaceX, led by Elon Musk, is a paragon of persistence and perseverance in the modern business landscape. The journey of SpaceX was marked by a series of setbacks, including multiple failed rocket launches, which could have easily led to the company's demise. However, under Musk's leadership, SpaceX maintained its focus and continued to push the boundaries of aerospace technology. Despite these early failures, the company persevered, learning from each setback and improving its designs and strategies. This relentless pursuit eventually led to groundbreaking achievements, including the successful launch of the Falcon 1 and the historic feat of becoming the first private company to send a spacecraft to the International Space Station. SpaceX's journey from a struggling startup to a leader in space exploration is a testament to the power of persistence and perseverance. It demonstrates how resilience, coupled with a clear vision and relentless effort, can overcome obstacles and lead to extraordinary achievements in any field.

## 4. Visionary Leadership

**Lesson from the Ramayana:** The construction of the bridge to Lanka in the Ramayana is a classic example of visionary leadership demonstrated by Lord Rama. This monumental task required not only physical resources but also a clear and compelling vision. Rama's foresight, strategic planning, and ability to inspire and rally diverse groups towards a common goal were instrumental in turning this daunting vision into a reality. His leadership transcended conventional thinking; he envisioned a solution that seemed unattainable and motivated his followers to achieve the extraordinary. Rama's approach illustrates how visionary leadership combines strategic foresight with the power to inspire and galvanize people towards a unified objective, even in the face of seemingly insurmountable odds.

**Modern Application:** In contemporary leadership, the ability to articulate and pursue a clear and compelling vision is crucial. Effective leaders must possess the foresight to anticipate future challenges and opportunities, formulate strategic plans, and inspire their teams to work towards these goals. This involves not only setting a clear direction but also motivating and guiding the team through the inevitable challenges and obstacles. A visionary leader is one who can see beyond the immediate horizon, imagine what could be, and then mobilize resources and people to turn that vision into reality. This kind of leadership is especially vital in times of change and uncertainty, where a clear sense of direction and purpose can provide much-needed stability and focus.

**Jeff Bezos Leads:**  Jeff Bezos, the founder and former CEO of Amazon, is a prime example of visionary leadership in action. When he started Amazon, Bezos had a clear and ambitious vision - to build the world's most customer-centric company, where people could find and discover anything they might want to buy online. This vision was far-reaching at a time when the internet and e-commerce were in their nascent stages. Bezos' foresight into the potential of online retail, coupled with his relentless focus on customer satisfaction, innovation, and long-term thinking, has been fundamental to Amazon's growth. He successfully led the company through various industry transformations, constantly adapting and innovating to stay ahead. Under his leadership, Amazon evolved from an online bookstore to a global e-commerce and cloud computing giant. Bezos' ability to envision a radically different future and his unwavering commitment to realizing this vision demonstrate the transformative power of visionary leadership.

## 5.  Adaptability and Flexibility

**Lesson from the Ramayana:**  The task of building the bridge to Lanka in the Ramayana is a profound lesson in adaptability and flexibility. Faced with the formidable challenge of crossing an ocean, Rama and his army had to be inventive, adaptive, and flexible in their approach. They adapted to varying terrains, weather conditions, and the sheer scale of the task at hand. This adaptability was not just in terms of physical construction but also in strategizing, managing resources, and overcoming unforeseen obstacles. Their ability to adjust plans, improvise solutions, and remain resilient in the face of adversity was crucial in turning the daunting vision into a successful reality. The Ramayana teaches that flexibility and adaptability are essential in achieving goals, especially when the path to success is fraught with challenges and uncertainties.

**Modern Application:**   In today's ever-evolving business landscape, adaptability and flexibility are more critical than ever. Organizations face a constant flux of market dynamics, technological advancements, and consumer behavior changes. Successful companies are those that can quickly pivot and adapt their strategies, business models, and operational processes in response to these changes. Being adaptable means staying open to new ideas, being willing to discard outdated practices, and continuously learning and evolving. This agility enables organizations to seize new opportunities, navigate through challenges, and remain competitive in a dynamic business environment.

**The Growth of Netflix:**   Netflix's evolution is a quintessential example of adaptability in the business world. Initially a DVD rental service, Netflix swiftly adapted its business model in response to the digital revolution and changing consumer preferences. Recognizing the potential of streaming technology and on-demand content, Netflix transitioned to become a streaming service, fundamentally changing how people consume entertainment. This pivot was not without risks, but Netflix's willingness to embrace change and innovate was key to its success. The company continually adapts, whether in content creation, distribution strategies, or exploring new technologies like AI for personalized viewing experiences. Netflix's journey from a DVD rental service to a global streaming powerhouse underscores the significance of adaptability and flexibility in achieving long-term success and relevance in a rapidly changing industry.

## Embracing Timeless Lessons from the Bridge to Lanka

The epic narrative of building the bridge to Lanka in the Ramayana is not just a story of a miraculous feat; it is a repository of timeless lessons that hold profound significance in today's complex leadership landscape. This legendary episode transcends its mythological roots, offering a rich panorama of insights into overcoming obstacles, a theme universally relevant across epochs and cultures.

**Collective Strength and Unity:** The construction of the bridge highlights the immense power of collaboration and unity. It exemplifies how bringing together diverse skills, perspectives, and strengths can surmount even the most daunting challenges. In the modern corporate world, this translates to fostering a culture of teamwork and inclusivity, where every member's contribution is valued and leveraged. The synergy of a united team, much like Rama's diverse army, can lead to extraordinary accomplishments and innovative solutions.

**Strategic Innovation and Problem-Solving:** The ingenuity in overcoming the engineering marvel of building a bridge across an ocean underscores the value of creative problem-solving and strategic innovation. Today, businesses and organizations face a plethora of challenges that require novel approaches and out-of-the-box thinking. Embracing innovation, just as Rama and his army did, is key to navigating and thriving in today's fast-paced and ever-changing environment.

**Persistence and Perseverance:** The relentless effort and unwavering commitment of Rama's army in building the bridge serve as a testament to the power of perseverance. This lesson is particularly resonant in today's world, where persistence in the face of setbacks and challenges is crucial for success. The spirit of perseverance, akin to that shown in the Ramayana, is essential for leaders and teams to realize their visions and goals.

**Visionary Leadership:** Lord Rama's leadership in envisioning and guiding the construction of the bridge is a prime example of visionary leadership. His ability to inspire and rally his followers towards a common goal is a lesson in effective leadership. Modern leaders can draw inspiration from Rama's example to articulate clear visions, inspire their teams, and lead them towards achieving shared objectives.

**Adaptability and Flexibility:** The adaptability and flexibility shown in overcoming various challenges during the bridge's construction are crucial traits for modern organizations. In an age characterized by rapid technological advances and market fluctuations, the ability to adapt and pivot strategies is vital for survival and growth. The Ramayana teaches us that flexibility and readiness to embrace change are key to navigating the complexities of the modern business landscape.

The bridge to Lanka, thus, serves as a metaphor for overcoming obstacles through collective effort, innovation, resilience, visionary leadership, and adaptability. These timeless lessons from the Ramayana are as relevant today as they were in the ancient epic. They provide a guiding framework for contemporary leaders and teams to approach their challenges with wisdom, creativity, and determination. By embracing these enduring principles, modern organizations can build their own bridges to success, transforming obstacles into stepping stones for achievement and growth.

# Chapter 9

# Wisdom from the Vanaras: Teamwork and Unity

The Vanaras, a tribe of agile and intelligent forest beings, emerge as striking symbols of teamwork and unity in the epic Ramayana. Their significant contributions, most notably in aiding Lord Rama during his arduous quest to rescue Sita, offer rich insights into collaborative success and the essence of collective strength. The Vanaras, characterized by their diverse abilities, unwavering dedication, and dynamic leadership, embody the principles of effective teamwork that resonate profoundly with contemporary organizational dynamics.Among these are the Vanaras, whose roles in the epic exemplify exceptional teamwork and unity. This chapter aims to delve deeper into their characteristics, shedding light on specific traits, their ability to handle internal conflicts, and the unique attributes of key figures like Hanuman, Sugriva, Angada, and Jambavan.

The Vanaras' story is a testament to several crucial aspects of effective team dynamics. Their resourcefulness in the quest to locate Sita and their steadfast commitment to Rama, even in the face of dire threats, exemplify a level of dedication and ingenuity that transcends mere cooperation. Each Vanara contributes distinct skills to the group's success, from Hanuman's immense strength and strategic acumen to Sugriva's leadership, Angada's bravery, and Jambavan's seasoned wisdom. This diversity of talents, meshing together in perfect harmony, is a crucial element of their triumph.

In addition to their strengths, the Vanaras also encounter internal disagreements and moments of doubt. This chapter will explore how they navigate these challenges to maintain unity, offering a realistic and relatable portrayal of team dynamics.

We will also take a closer look at key events such as the meticulous search for Sita, which showcases the Vanaras' commitment and problem-solving skills. The construction of the bridge to Lanka, a monumental task, will be described in vivid detail, underscoring the importance of each Vanara's unique abilities and the collective triumph over adversity. This symbol of overcoming obstacles through united effort is a powerful metaphor for the challenges modern teams face.

The chapter will bridge these ancient lessons with modern-day applications, offering practical strategies and real-world examples of teams that have successfully implemented the Vanaras' principles. By drawing parallels between the challenges faced by the Vanaras and those in contemporary organizations, we aim to provide actionable insights for today's leaders and teams. From fostering open communication and leveraging individual strengths to resolving conflicts constructively, this chapter will serve as a guide for harnessing the power of teamwork and unity, inspired by the wisdom of the Vanaras.

# The Power of Collective Effort: Harnessing Team Strength in Unity

### *Lesson from the Ramayana*

The Vanaras' mission, encompassing the search for Sita and the construction of the bridge to Lanka, was an extraordinary display of teamwork. The story illustrates not merely the triumph of individual heroes but a symphony of varied talents working in harmony towards a common goal. This successful outcome was the result of every Vanara, from the humblest to the most esteemed, contributing their unique abilities and strengths. It was a collaborative venture where individual skills were not just combined but amplified through the spirit of teamwork.

Hanuman, the embodiment of strength and devotion, provided much more than physical prowess. His unparalleled agility, strategic thinking, and deep dedication to Rama's cause were instrumental in overcoming numerous challenges. Nala, another key figure among the Vanaras, utilized his architectural and engineering skills to mastermind the construction of the bridge. His knowledge and technical expertise were crucial in turning an ambitious plan into a feasible reality.

Jambavan, the wise elder of the tribe, offered invaluable counsel and guidance throughout the journey. His experience and wisdom helped navigate the team through difficult decisions and strategy formulation. Sugriva, the king of the Vanaras, led with strategic acumen and motivational leadership, ensuring the collective efforts were focused and effective.

This diverse array of talents and abilities among the Vanaras was unified under a shared vision – to assist Rama in his quest. Their collaboration highlights how differences in skill and perspective, when aligned towards a singular objective, can lead to extraordinary accomplishments. The narrative beautifully encapsulates the essence of teamwork: that true strength lies not in individual prowess alone but in the collective power of a united group working towards a shared goal.

In the modern context, the story of the Vanaras serves as a powerful metaphor for organizational teamwork and collaborative effort. It underscores the value of diverse skills and perspectives in a team and the importance of aligning these individual strengths towards a common objective. The saga of the Vanaras in the Ramayana thus becomes a timeless lesson in teamwork, unity, and the power of collective endeavor.

## Modern Application

In the context of contemporary organizations, the Vanaras' approach to teamwork holds invaluable lessons. It emphasizes the significance of acknowledging and integrating each individual's unique skills and perspectives. Modern leaders can draw inspiration from this model by creating a culture that celebrates diversity and encourages collaborative synergy. It's about crafting an environment where different talents are not just welcomed but are seen as crucial components of the team's success. Encouraging open communication, fostering mutual respect, and aligning individual goals with the organization's objectives are key to replicating this model of teamwork in modern-day settings.

## Harmony in Adversity:   The Tham Luang Cave Rescue

The dramatic rescue of the Thai soccer team from the depths of the Tham Luang cave in 2018 stands as a modern testament to the power of teamwork and unity, reminiscent of the collaborative efforts of the Vanaras in the Ramayana. This real-life saga unfolded in northern Thailand, where a young soccer team and their coach were trapped deep within a flooded cave system, presenting a rescue challenge of unprecedented complexity and danger.

Like the diverse abilities of the Vanaras, the rescue operation brought together a unique blend of skills from across the globe. The team comprised Thai Navy SEALs, who brought their expertise in tactical operations and underwater navigation. They were joined by the world's best cave divers, individuals who had honed their skills in some of the most challenging underwater environments on earth. These divers brought with them a deep understanding of the cave's labyrinthine layout and the perils associated with cave diving.

Medical professionals, both on-site and remote, played a crucial role. They assessed the health and wellbeing of the trapped team, strategized their safe extraction, and provided immediate medical care. The rescue also saw engineers and water management experts who were instrumental in devising strategies to pump out the floodwaters and stabilize the cave environment.

The support teams, comprising local volunteers, government agencies, and international groups, were the unsung heroes. They managed logistics, maintained communication lines, and ensured a steady supply of essential resources. The local community rallied together, providing food and moral support, while experts from around the world contributed their knowledge and experience.

This extraordinary rescue operation was marked by a level of international cooperation and unity rarely seen. Each individual and team brought their unique strengths to the fore, but it was their ability to work in harmony, adapting to rapidly changing situations, that was pivotal in the success of the mission. The operation required not only technical expertise but also immense trust, coordination, and emotional strength.

The Tham Luang cave rescue, like the story of the Vanaras, exemplifies how diverse talents and strengths, when united by a common goal, can achieve what seems impossible. It is a vivid illustration of how collaboration, adaptability, and collective strength can prevail over daunting challenges, providing a powerful lesson in unity and teamwork in the face of adversity.

## Leadership and Coordination

### *Lesson from the Ramayana*

In the Ramayana, the successful endeavors of the Vanaras, especially in the search for Sita and the construction of the bridge to Lanka, are a testament to the effective leadership of Sugriva and the exemplary coordination by Hanuman. Their roles in these monumental tasks were not just about issuing orders; it was about inspiring a diverse team, understanding individual strengths, and harnessing these for a unified purpose.

Sugriva's leadership was characterized by his strategic acumen and ability to galvanize the Vanaras towards a common goal. As a king, he demonstrated a profound understanding of each member's capabilities, assigning tasks that aligned with their unique skills. This effective delegation was crucial in maximizing the efficiency and impact of the team's efforts. Sugriva's leadership shone not just in his strategic planning but also in his ability to instill confidence and hope in his followers, especially in moments of doubt and uncertainty. His ability to keep the morale high and maintain a focused direction was key in navigating through the challenging journey.

Hanuman, as Sugriva's chief aide, played a critical role in coordinating these efforts. His exceptional qualities - strength, intelligence, resourcefulness, and unwavering loyalty - made him an ideal figure to lead and rally the troops. Hanuman's role went beyond mere execution of tasks; he was instrumental in bridging the gap between Sugriva's commands and the team's actions. His ability to communicate effectively, inspire his peers, and lead by example was pivotal in maintaining the coherence and unity of the team. Hanuman's approach to coordination was not authoritarian; it was inclusive, empathetic, and adaptive to the dynamics of the situation.

The collaborative leadership of Sugriva and the adept coordination by Hanuman created a synergy that was the driving force behind the Vanaras' success. Their approach highlights the importance of strategic leadership and effective coordination in achieving complex objectives. It underscores the value of understanding and leveraging individual strengths, fostering clear communication, and maintaining morale through challenging times.

In modern organizational settings, this narrative from the Ramayana offers invaluable lessons in leadership and team management. It emphasizes the need for leaders to recognize and utilize the diverse talents within their teams, to communicate objectives clearly, and to inspire and motivate their members towards common goals. Sugriva's strategic leadership coupled with Hanuman's effective coordination serves as a blueprint for building and steering successful teams in any field, demonstrating that with the right leadership and coordination, even the most daunting challenges can be overcome.

### *Modern Application*

Effective leadership and coordination are crucial in any team setting. Leaders must inspire confidence, delegate tasks appropriately, and maintain open communication. Coordinating team efforts to ensure that everyone is working synergistically towards a shared objective is key.

### Uniting for a Milestone:   The Human Genome Project

The Human Genome Project (HGP) stands as a quintessential example of global coordination and leadership, mirroring the essence of teamwork and strategic guidance seen in the Ramayana's depiction of the Vanaras. Initiated in 1990 and completed in 2003, this groundbreaking project aimed to map and understand all the genes of human beings, a task as monumental and complex as the challenges faced by the Vanaras in the Ramayana.

The project's success was rooted in its unprecedented scale of international collaboration. It involved thousands of scientists, bioethicists, legal experts, and technicians across various countries, including the United States, the United Kingdom, Japan, France, Germany, and China. This diverse group brought together a multitude of perspectives, expertise, and techniques, much like the Vanaras under Sugriva's leadership utilized their unique abilities for a common goal.

Leadership and coordination were crucial in the HGP, as they were in the Vanaras' mission. The project was steered by visionary leaders who recognized the importance of pooling global knowledge and resources. They had to navigate not only scientific and technical challenges but also ethical, legal, and social implications. This required not only scientific acumen but also diplomatic skills to foster cooperation among various national and international institutions.

The project leaders also had to ensure effective communication and data sharing among the diverse groups involved, a task akin to Hanuman's role in coordinating the Vanaras' efforts. This was crucial in maintaining the project's pace and coherence. The establishment of data-sharing policies that allowed free access to the information gathered by the project was a significant step in ensuring transparency and collaboration, driving the project towards its successful completion.

The completion of the Human Genome Project is a testament to what can be achieved through collaborative effort, strategic planning, and effective leadership. It has laid the foundation for numerous advances in genetics, medicine, and biotechnology, much like the Vanaras' efforts led to the successful rescue of Sita. The HGP is a modern example of how unity, diversity of skills, and effective coordination can lead to achieving seemingly impossible milestones.

The Human Genome Project serves as a modern parallel to the strategic and coordinated efforts of the Vanaras in the Ramayana. It exemplifies how visionary leadership, coupled with global collaboration and effective communication, can overcome colossal challenges. This example continues to inspire and guide current and future large-scale collaborative endeavors, demonstrating the power and potential of united efforts in achieving groundbreaking achievements.

## Overcoming Differences for a Common Goal: Enhanced Unity in Diversity

### *Lesson from the Ramayana*

The tale of the Vanaras assembling to aid Lord Rama illustrates a profound lesson in overcoming individual differences to achieve a collective goal. The Vanaras, despite having varied backgrounds, strengths, and personalities, united under the common purpose of finding Sita and defeating Ravana. This unity was not merely about setting aside personal differences; it was about recognizing and respecting these differences to create a stronger, more cohesive force.

The Vanaras' story shows the power of a shared vision in bringing together disparate individuals. Leaders like Sugriva and Hanuman played crucial roles in aligning these diverse characters towards a singular goal. They acknowledged and valued the unique contributions of each Vanara, whether it was Hanuman's unparalleled strength, Nala's architectural ingenuity, or Jambavan's sage advice. This inclusive approach fostered a sense of belonging and purpose among the team members, driving them to work harmoniously despite their differences.

Moreover, the Vanaras' story is a testament to the importance of emotional intelligence in leadership. Recognizing and managing not just one's own emotions but also those of the team members was crucial in maintaining unity amidst diversity. The leaders' ability to understand and address individual concerns, motivations, and aspirations ensured that the collective morale remained high, even in the face of daunting challenges.

In today's world, where teams often consist of individuals from varied cultural, professional, and personal backgrounds, the lesson from the Vanaras is particularly relevant. Embracing diversity, fostering an inclusive environment, and rallying everyone around a common goal are essential leadership qualities. The Vanaras' example shows that when differences are not just tolerated but valued and leveraged, they become a source of strength and innovation, driving the team towards achieving remarkable feats.

This lesson from the Ramayana can be a guiding principle for modern leaders: to recognize diversity as an asset, to foster an environment where every team member feels valued, and to harness these diverse perspectives towards achieving a shared vision.

### Modern Application

In a diverse workplace, it's vital to foster an inclusive culture where differences are respected and leveraged for the team's benefit. Emphasizing common goals can help in overcoming personal conflicts and building a more cohesive team.

### Embracing Collaboration Beyond Rivalry: The Apple-IBM Partnership

The landmark collaboration between Apple Inc. and IBM, once arch-rivals in the tech industry, exemplifies the remarkable outcomes achievable when erstwhile competitors unite for a common goal. This partnership, initiated in 2014, was a strategic alliance aimed at transforming enterprise mobility through the development of business applications for iOS users.

The Apple-IBM collaboration marked a significant shift in the business strategies of both companies. For years, Apple and IBM had been at opposite ends of the technology spectrum, with Apple focusing on consumer electronics and IBM on enterprise computing. This alliance was not just a business move; it was a symbolic bridging of two distinct corporate cultures and histories.

The partnership leveraged the strengths of both companies: Apple's innovative edge in user-friendly device interfaces and IBM's deep roots in enterprise computing and data analytics. Together, they aimed to create a suite of apps that could bring the simplicity and intuitiveness of Apple's user experience to complex business processes, thereby revolutionizing enterprise mobility.

One of the key elements of this partnership was the development of IBM MobileFirst for iOS solutions – a series of industry-specific apps designed to transform enterprise mobility. These apps combined IBM's big data and analytics capabilities with Apple's consumer experience, creating powerful tools for businesses in sectors ranging from healthcare to banking.

The collaboration also involved IBM selling iPhones and iPads loaded with enterprise solutions to its business clients, thus expanding Apple's reach in the corporate sector. Moreover, IBM provided cloud services optimized for iOS, ensuring efficient and secure functioning of these devices and applications in enterprise settings.

This alliance between Apple and IBM is a vivid illustration of how former competitors can find common ground and create synergies that benefit both parties. It demonstrates that by setting aside past rivalries and focusing on mutual strengths, companies can open new avenues for innovation and growth. The Apple-IBM partnership not only led to groundbreaking products but also signaled a new era of cooperation in the technology industry, showing that even the fiercest of competitors can unite to forge paths to shared success.

## Celebrating Individual Contributions Within Team Goals

### *Lesson from the Ramayana*

The victory of the Vanaras, a tribe of forest-dwellers, in assisting Lord Rama is often lauded as a testament to their collective strength. However, an in-depth examination of this triumph reveals a rich fabric of individual feats and distinct contributions. The Vanaras, led by Sugriva and inspired by Rama, displayed an exemplary blend of unity and individual prowess.

Each member of the Vanara tribe brought their unique abilities to the forefront, contributing indispensably to the mission. Hanuman's legendary leap to Lanka is not just a display of physical strength; it is a symbol of courage, commitment, and strategic acumen. His journey was fraught with challenges, yet his determination and faith in Rama's cause never wavered. On the other hand, Nala, the son of the divine architect Vishwakarma, utilized his inherited architectural skills to design and construct the bridge to Lanka. This monumental task, achieved through innovative engineering and teamwork, stands as a marvel of the Vanaras' collective endeavor.

The diversity within the Vanara ranks was vast, ranging from the elderly wisdom of Jambavan to the youthful vigor of Angada. Each Vanara, irrespective of their rank and capabilities, played a significant role. Their distinct contributions, whether in planning, combat, or support, were crucial in advancing Rama's mission.

This harmonious blend of individual excellence and team spirit in the Ramayana imparts a profound lesson in team dynamics and leadership. It illustrates how recognizing and celebrating individual talents within a team can amplify collective success. Leaders can draw inspiration from this narrative by fostering an environment where every team member's unique contribution is acknowledged and valued. Such recognition not only enhances team morale but also cultivates a sense of ownership and pride in each member, driving them to contribute their best towards the team's objectives.

In essence, the Ramayana teaches us that while unity and collaboration are the bedrocks of a successful team, the individual talents and efforts within the team are like precious gems that, when polished and rightly placed, can create a masterpiece of collective achievement.

## Modern Application

In contemporary workplaces, leaders can take inspiration from this lesson by creating an environment that values individual contributions as much as team achievements. This involves recognizing and celebrating the unique skills and efforts each team member brings. Whether it's a creative solution, diligent work, or exceptional leadership, acknowledging these contributions fosters a sense of belonging and appreciation among team members. It also encourages a culture of excellence where individuals are motivated to contribute their best, knowing that their efforts will be recognized and valued.

## Innovation through Individuality: Google's Blueprint for Team Success

Google's unique approach to team management and project development presents a compelling modern-day example that mirrors the lesson of celebrating individuality within team unity, as exemplified by the Vanaras in the Ramayana. This tech giant, renowned for its innovative and forward-thinking work environment, has long encouraged its employees to engage in 'passion projects' alongside their core responsibilities. This policy, often termed as the '20% time', allows team members to dedicate a portion of their work hours to exploring new ideas and personal interests that may benefit the company.

This innovative approach has led to the creation of some of Google's most groundbreaking and successful products. Gmail, for instance, originated from a passion project. It revolutionized email usage with its user-friendly interface and large storage capacity, significantly outperforming existing services at the time. Similarly, Google News, another brainchild born out of an employee's personal project, aggregated news from various sources, significantly changing how people consumed news online.

By valuing and nurturing the individual talents and interests of its employees within the company's broader objectives, Google has created an ecosystem of innovation and creativity. Employees are motivated to explore and experiment, knowing that their personal contributions and ideas are not only welcomed but also essential to the company's growth and evolution. This culture of acknowledging and celebrating individual ingenuity has not only led to the development of novel products and services but has also fostered a sense of belonging and investment among the workforce.

Google's strategy exemplifies how a company can successfully harness the unique skills and passions of its individual team members while aligning them with collective goals. This approach resonates with the dynamic synergy of the Vanaras, where each member's distinct abilities and efforts were integral to their collective mission. By creating an environment where individual creativity is valued and cultivated, Google mirrors the Ramayana's timeless lesson on the power of combining individual excellence with team collaboration to achieve remarkable success.

The saga of the Vanaras in the Ramayana, rich in allegorical depth, offers profound lessons in teamwork, leadership, and organizational success that are remarkably pertinent in today's complex professional landscape. From the unified effort in building the bridge to Lanka to their strategic and resourceful approach in locating Sita, the Vanaras epitomize the essence of effective collaboration, innovative problem-solving, and the strength of diversity.

This ancient narrative, when viewed through the lens of modern organizational principles, underscores several key aspects essential for contemporary leadership and team dynamics. Firstly, the power of collective effort, as exemplified by the diverse but unified Vanara army, teaches us the importance of harnessing the varied skills and strengths of team members. It highlights that when diverse talents are aligned towards a shared goal, the results can surpass expectations and lead to groundbreaking achievements, as seen in the collaborative efforts of the International Space Station or the innovative environment of Google.

Furthermore, the leadership styles of Sugriva and Hanuman provide valuable insights into the roles of visionary and coordinative leadership. Their ability to guide, inspire, and effectively utilize the diverse capabilities of their team members resonates with the leadership approaches needed to steer modern organizations towards success. This is mirrored in the strategic and inclusive leadership displayed by figures like Jeff Bezos of Amazon, who transformed the retail landscape with his visionary approach.

The narrative also brings to light the significance of overcoming differences for a common objective. The Vanaras, despite their varied backgrounds and personal traits, united for a cause greater than themselves. This unity in diversity, paralleling alliances like that of Apple and IBM, serves as a powerful reminder of the strength that lies in setting aside differences to achieve shared visions.

Moreover, the story of the Vanaras celebrates individual contributions within the collective framework. It acknowledges that while teamwork is crucial, recognizing and valuing individual efforts is equally important for maintaining morale and fostering innovation. This balance between individual recognition and team success is crucial in creating an environment where each member feels valued and motivated, as exemplified by Google's approach to employee innovation.

The wisdom encapsulated in the tale of the Vanaras extends beyond the realm of mythological lore, offering tangible, applicable lessons for modern-day leadership and teamwork. By integrating these timeless principles — collective strength, visionary leadership, embracing diversity, and valuing individual contributions — contemporary leaders and teams can navigate the complexities of their professional environments more effectively. The Vanaras' story is not just a narrative of mythical heroism; it is a blueprint for building resilient, innovative, and successful teams in today's ever-evolving world.

# Chapter 10

# The Final Battle: Conquering Inner Demons

In the sprawling epic of the Ramayana, a tale that has captured the imagination and guided the moral compass of generations, there lies a deeply resonant chapter - "The Final Battle: Conquering Inner Demons." This chapter illuminates the profound internal struggles faced by Lord Rama, a paragon of virtue and an embodiment of divine strength, in his climactic confrontation with Ravana. More than a mere battle against an external foe, this chapter delves into Rama's confrontation with his inner demons, symbolizing a universal human experience of battling personal doubts, fears, anger, and temptations.

This narrative transcends the physical skirmishes on the battlegrounds of Lanka, venturing into the more nuanced and often tumultuous realm of internal conflict. Here, Rama, often revered as an infallible deity, is portrayed in his most human light, grappling with vulnerabilities and moral dilemmas that resonate deeply with the human psyche. This chapter is an exploration of the complexities of the human spirit, where even a figure of Rama's stature is not immune to the trials and tribulations that accompany introspection and self-doubt.

Through a detailed analysis of key moments in the Ramayana, this chapter will unravel the layers of Rama's internal battle. It will probe into how moments of self-doubt and moral questioning are not signs of weakness, but rather stepping stones to greater understanding and self-mastery. The narrative will dissect how these inner conflicts are as formidable as the external ones, and how Rama's journey of confronting and overcoming them is as heroic as his battle against Ravana.

At its core, "The Final Battle: Conquering Inner Demons" is not just a recounting of an ancient myth but a mirror reflecting the perennial struggle within each individual. It brings forth the concept that the toughest battles are often fought within the confines of one's mind and soul. This chapter, therefore, is a guide, a source of comfort, and a beacon of hope for anyone who has ever faced the daunting task of confronting their inner demons. It offers not just a narrative but also practical wisdom on how to navigate these internal battles, drawing strength from virtues of righteousness, ethics, and the power of introspection.

As much as it is a tale of ancient lore, this chapter is a testament to the timeless nature of the Ramayana's teachings. It exemplifies how the epic's lessons continue to be relevant, offering insights and strategies that are applicable in the modern world's complex landscape of ethical dilemmas and emotional challenges.

## Internal Struggle as the Truest Battle

### *Lesson from the Ramayana*

The iconic battle between Lord Rama and Ravana transcends its physical dimensions, emerging as a profound allegory for the internal skirmishes we all face. This confrontation is not just a battle for the rescue of Sita; it's a canvas where Rama, embodying human virtues, grapples with his internal turmoil. This narrative layer adds a complex dimension to Rama's character, painting him not just as a divine figure but as a relatable human being wrestling with doubts and fears. The conflict with Ravana, therefore, becomes a dual battle – one that is fought on the battleground of Lanka and the other, perhaps more formidable, within the depths of Rama's conscience.

Rama's internal struggles are manifold. They include his doubts about his ability to rescue Sita, the weight of the expectations placed upon him, and the moral dilemmas he faces. These inner conflicts are as arduous as the physical war he wages. The narrative delves into moments where Rama questions his decisions, feels the weight of the moral choices he must make, and confronts the shadows of fear and uncertainty. This introspection and self-questioning add layers to his character, making him a multifaceted hero whose true strength lies in overcoming these internal adversities.

Ravana, in this context, represents more than a physical antagonist; he is the embodiment of the darker forces within Rama – the temptations, the rage, the thirst for vengeance. Each of Ravana's ten heads can be seen as a symbol of these vices and inner demons that Rama must conquer. The battle, therefore, is emblematic of Rama's journey to overcome these negative forces, to adhere to dharma (righteous duty) despite the provocations and challenges posed by these internal enemies.

### Modern Application

In today's world, the battle against one's inner demons is as relevant as ever. Leaders and individuals in various spheres encounter situations where they must confront their personal doubts, ethical dilemmas, and moral weaknesses. This internal struggle can manifest as a conflict between professional ambition and personal values, the temptation to take shortcuts for quick success, or the challenge of maintaining integrity under pressure. The lesson here is the recognition that the most significant victories are those won within oneself. Success, in its truest form, is defined by the ability to uphold one's values and principles, especially when they are tested.

## *Triumph Over Adversity*

The story of Malala Yousafzai resonates deeply with the allegorical narrative of Rama's internal battle in the Ramayana. Malala's struggle against the forces of oppression and her fight for education rights in Pakistan mirror the metaphorical battle within Rama - a confrontation between courage and fear, between conviction and surrender. Her journey is not just a physical struggle against the tangible threats posed by the Taliban but also an internal battle against fear, despair, and the temptation to relinquish her fight in the face of overwhelming adversity.

At a young age, Malala faced challenges that tested not only her physical endurance but also her mental fortitude. After surviving a life-threatening attack for her advocacy, the path to recovery and continuing her crusade was fraught with fear, pain, and uncertainty. Malala's internal struggle involved overcoming the natural fear for personal safety and the emotional turmoil following the traumatic experience. Despite these challenges, her unwavering commitment to her cause – the right to education for girls – remained steadfast. Malala's resilience in this regard is akin to Rama's perseverance in his internal battle, demonstrating a remarkable strength of character and an unyielding adherence to her principles.

In Malala's story, the Taliban can be seen as a modern-day Ravana, symbolizing the forces of darkness and oppression.

Malala's defiance and resolve in the face of this adversary highlight her internal victory over fear and intimidation. Her courage, much like Rama's, becomes a beacon of hope and a symbol of the triumph of good over evil, of light over darkness.

Malala's narrative is not just a tale of survival; it is a powerful example of how unwavering conviction can lead to significant change. Despite the physical and psychological scars, she continued to use her voice to advocate for education, becoming the youngest-ever Nobel Prize laureate. Her journey from a young girl in the Swat Valley to an international symbol of peaceful protest and the power of education is a testament to the human spirit's ability to conquer inner demons and effect change.

## Embracing Self-Awareness: Rama's Acknowledgment of Inner Demons

### *Lesson from the Ramayana*

In the intricate narrative of the Ramayana, the confrontation between Lord Rama and Ravana extends far beyond a physical duel. It encapsulates a profound, introspective journey where Rama, despite his divine lineage, confronts and grapples with his human emotions and doubts. This duality in Rama's character is pivotal in understanding the essence of conquering inner demons.

Rama, revered as an incarnation of the divine, is not impervious to the spectrum of human emotions. He faces moments of self-doubt, moral ambiguity, and internal conflict, making his character multifaceted and deeply human. These instances are critical, as they bring forth his vulnerabilities, painting a picture of a hero who is relatable in his struggles. Rama's internal battle with these emotions is as significant as his external struggles, highlighting a key aspect of the human condition: the internal turmoil we all face at various points in our lives.

Throughout the Ramayana, Rama's journey is not only about defeating the external adversary in Ravana but also about introspection and mastering his inner world. His acknowledgment of his fears, doubts, and emotional upheavals is an essential part of his character arc. This self-awareness is a form of humility and strength, as it is the first step toward overcoming personal challenges. Rama's introspection leads him to understand his vulnerabilities, accept them, and eventually transcend them, thereby achieving a sense of inner harmony and strength.

The story of Rama, then, becomes a powerful lesson in the importance of self-reflection and the courage to face one's inner demons. It teaches that true bravery and wisdom lie not just in conquering external challenges but in the ability to confront and overcome our deepest fears and doubts. This inner journey of self-realization and mastery is what truly defines Rama's character and elevates him as a timeless example of strength and resilience.

## Modern Application

In contemporary times, the recognition and acknowledgment of one's inner demons are crucial for personal and professional development. In a world that often prioritizes external achievements and appearances, Rama's example encourages individuals to look inward, confront their fears and doubts, and embark on a journey of self-discovery and improvement. It's a reminder that true strength lies in acknowledging one's weaknesses and working towards overcoming them.

## The Oprah Effect: Embracing Inner Challenges for Personal Mastery

Oprah Winfrey's life journey offers a contemporary reflection of Lord Rama's internal battle, as depicted in the Ramayana. Like

Rama, Oprah's story is one of confronting and overcoming inner demons, a narrative that speaks volumes about the universal nature of such struggles and the transformative power of self-awareness and personal growth.

Oprah Winfrey, a globally recognized media mogul, philanthropist, and influencer, has faced numerous challenges throughout her life and career. Rising from a background marked by poverty, abuse, and racial discrimination, her path to success was fraught with obstacles. However, her struggles extended beyond these external barriers. Oprah grappled with deep-seated internal conflicts – from battling self-doubt and body image issues to dealing with the emotional scars of her traumatic childhood experiences. These internal battles were as significant in shaping her character and destiny as her external triumphs.

Oprah's willingness to openly share her personal struggles has been a hallmark of her public persona. She has spoken candidly about her journey through therapy and self-exploration, highlighting the importance of confronting one's past and emotional pain. Her transparency in discussing these issues has not only humanized her but also made her an icon of resilience and personal transformation.

Her career, marked by groundbreaking achievements in television, literature, and philanthropy, is underscored by her continual quest for personal growth. Oprah's talk show, book club, and network have often focused on themes of self-improvement, emotional well-being, and spiritual growth, reflecting her commitment to these values in her personal life. Through her platforms, she has encouraged millions to embark on their journeys of self-discovery and healing.

Oprah Winfrey's life serves as a modern-day parallel to Rama's introspective journey in the Ramayana. It demonstrates that the conquest of inner demons through self-awareness, acceptance, and personal development is a potent force. Her story resonates with the timeless lesson from the epic: true mastery and fulfillment come not only from external achievements but from conquering the internal struggles that define the human experience.

## Harnessing Inner Strength and Righteousness

### *Lesson from the Ramayana*

The essence of Lord Rama's character is deeply intertwined with his steadfast commitment to dharma (righteousness) and the immense inner strength he draws from it. His adherence to ethical principles and moral courage are not just qualities but potent weapons in his arsenal, especially when confronting his inner demons and the external antagonist, Ravana. This chapter will delve deeply into how Rama's moral fortitude and unyielding commitment to righteousness empower him to face and overcome not only the physical challenges posed by Ravana but also the internal struggles that threaten his resolve.

Rama's journey is replete with instances where his commitment to dharma is tested. From choosing to honor his father's word and go into exile to facing the moral dilemma of fighting against Ravana, Rama consistently places dharma at the forefront of his decisions. This unwavering dedication to righteousness, even in the face of personal loss and emotional turmoil, is what distinguishes him. It's a testament to the strength that can be derived from a deep sense of ethical conviction and moral clarity. Rama's inner strength is a beacon that guides him through the darkest moments, providing clarity and purpose when faced with difficult choices.

Moreover, Rama's journey highlights that true inner strength is not the absence of doubt or fear, but the ability to confront and rise above these challenges by staying true to one's principles. His actions demonstrate that moral courage is not just about making the right choices but also about facing the consequences of these choices with integrity and resilience. This aspect of Rama's character sheds light on the transformative power of righteousness and ethical conviction in personal growth and overcoming life's trials.

### Modern Application

In today's fast-paced and often morally ambiguous world, the application of Rama's adherence to righteousness is profoundly relevant. Leaders and individuals in any field can draw inspiration from Rama's ethical conviction. This involves making decisions that are not just beneficial but are also rooted in moral integrity. It's about prioritizing ethical considerations over expedient choices, especially in challenging situations. Emulating Rama's approach means fostering a culture of integrity and accountability, where ethical principles guide actions and decisions. This approach is crucial in building trust and credibility, both within an organization and in its external relations. It also serves as a foundation for sustainable success and a positive social impact, as decisions grounded in ethical principles are more likely to yield long-term benefits and foster a culture of respect and responsibility.

### Nelson Mandela

Nelson Mandela's journey, which mirrors Lord Rama's adherence to dharma in the Ramayana, is a compelling testament to the power of righteousness and moral courage in the modern world. His struggle against the abhorrent system of apartheid in South Africa was not just a political battle; it was a moral crusade grounded in a deep commitment to justice and equality. Mandela's journey was marked by immense personal sacrifices, including spending 27 years in prison, often under harsh conditions. Yet, even in the depths of his incarceration, he never wavered from his ethical convictions.

Mandela's resilience and unyielding dedication to his principles were instrumental in dismantling South Africa's institutionalized racism. His leadership, characterized by moral strength and unwavering resolve, played a pivotal role in ending apartheid and ushering in a new era of democracy in the nation. Mandela's approach to leadership was not just about achieving political victory; it was about setting a moral example, about showing that ethical leadership and adherence to one's principles can effect real, meaningful change.

Even more remarkable was Mandela's commitment to forgiveness and reconciliation in the post-apartheid era. After enduring decades of injustice, he emerged without bitterness, advocating for unity and understanding among all South Africans. This aspect of his leadership – the ability to forgive and seek reconciliation – was a profound display of moral fortitude and humanity, resonating deeply with Rama's sense of righteousness in the Ramayana.

Mandela's life story is a powerful example of how adherence to ethical principles and moral courage can lead to significant societal transformations. His journey offers invaluable lessons in ethical leadership, demonstrating that true strength lies in staying true to one's principles and ideals, even in the face of adversity. Mandela's legacy continues to serve as a beacon of hope and inspiration, showing that righteousness and ethical conviction can lead to a better, more just world.

## Support Systems in the Battle Against Inner Demons

### Lesson from the Ramayana

In the critical moments of Lord Rama's journey in the Ramayana, his success against external adversaries and internal conflicts was significantly bolstered by the unwavering support of key allies like Hanuman, Lakshmana, and the Vanara army. This aspect of the epic underscores a vital lesson in dealing with internal struggles: the indispensable role of a robust support system.

Lord Rama's relationship with Hanuman, Lakshmana, and the Vanaras went beyond mere assistance in the physical battles. These allies provided emotional and moral support, serving as pillars of strength during Rama's moments of self-doubt and moral dilemma. Hanuman's unfaltering faith, Lakshmana's constant companionship and counsel, and the Vanaras' collective might and loyalty were crucial in bolstering Rama's resolve and aiding him in his internal and external battles.

In the contemporary context, this translates to the critical importance of nurturing supportive relationships – be it with mentors, friends, family, or professional allies. Just as Rama's supporters played diverse roles – offering wisdom, emotional support, and practical assistance – a well-rounded support system in our lives can provide varied and essential forms of support. Mentors and guides can offer wisdom and perspective, friends can lend a listening ear and emotional support, while family can provide a foundation of unconditional love and reassurance.

Especially when battling internal demons like anxiety, self-doubt, or burnout, the role of a supportive network becomes invaluable. In these moments, having someone to confide in, seek advice from, or simply stand by us can make a significant difference. This support system acts as a mirror reflecting our strengths when we are blinded by our struggles and serves as a reminder of our goals and values when we are swayed by internal conflicts.

The presence of a support system is akin to the silent yet powerful presence of Hanuman and Lakshmana by Rama's side. It is about having those who believe in us even when we doubt ourselves, those who offer a different perspective to our problems, and those who stand with us as we face our inner battles. The strength derived from this support is immeasurable and often becomes the deciding factor in our journey towards overcoming personal challenges and achieving self-mastery.

Thus, cultivating and cherishing these relationships in our personal and professional lives is not just beneficial but essential. It is about recognizing that the journey to conquering inner demons is not a solitary one but a path best navigated with the support, guidance, and companionship of others.

## *Modern Application*

In today's fast-paced and often high-pressure environment, cultivating a robust support system is crucial for personal and professional success. The modern application of this lesson involves actively seeking and nurturing relationships that provide emotional, intellectual, and moral support. This can take various forms:

- **Mentorship and Guidance:** Seeking mentors in one's field or area of interest who can provide advice, share experiences, and offer a broader perspective on challenges.

- **Peer Support:** Building a network of peers who understand the specific challenges of one's profession or life situation can offer invaluable support. Peer groups, either within an organization or in broader professional communities, can serve as a forum for sharing experiences and strategies for overcoming obstacles.

- **Family and Friends:** Maintaining strong ties with family and friends who provide emotional grounding and perspective outside of one's professional life. This support is essential for maintaining balance and resilience.

- **Professional Help:** Recognizing when professional help, such as therapy or counseling, is needed to navigate personal struggles effectively.

- **Online Communities:** Leveraging online platforms and communities for support, especially when facing niche or specific challenges where immediate physical support networks might be limited.

## The Power of Support

J.K. Rowling's ascent to becoming one of the most successful authors in history is a tale marked by perseverance, resilience, and the crucial role of a supportive network. Before the world knew her as the creator of "Harry Potter," Rowling faced a series of daunting personal challenges. As a single mother living on welfare, struggling to make ends meet, her situation seemed bleak. Her manuscript for "Harry Potter and the Philosopher's Stone" faced numerous rejections from publishers, adding to her trials.

Despite these setbacks, Rowling's journey was buoyed by a small but significant support system. This network included a few close friends and family members who believed in her potential when the odds were stacked against her. They provided not just emotional comfort but also practical assistance – whether it was encouraging words, taking care of her daughter while she wrote, or simply being a listening ear to her frustrations and fears.

A turning point came when Rowling met her literary agent, who saw the potential in her manuscript and advocated for her work with unwavering belief. This professional support was a crucial catalyst in her journey, transforming her manuscript from repeated rejections to a publishing success.

Rowling's story is also about finding solidarity and encouragement in a community of fellow writers. Engaging with peers who shared similar aspirations and struggles provided her with a sense of belonging and understanding. This community offered a platform for sharing experiences, learning, and drawing inspiration, which was instrumental in sustaining her motivation.

Rowling's experience highlights the multifaceted nature of support systems. It shows how different forms of support – emotional, practical, professional, and communal – can collectively contribute to overcoming challenges. Her story is a testament to the fact that while talent and perseverance are crucial, the support of others plays a pivotal role in navigating the path to success.

Rowling's journey from a struggling writer to a best-selling author exemplifies the transformative power of having a strong support system. It mirrors the support Rama received from his allies, emphasizing that even in the loneliest and most challenging times, the strength drawn from others can be a significant force in conquering adversities. Her story serves as an inspiration, showcasing how external support can enhance inner strength and resilience, and how the journey to success, much like Rama's epic quest, is often a collaborative effort.

This narrative of J.K. Rowling's triumph against adversity, underscored by the unwavering support she received, offers profound insights into the impact of a nurturing support system in personal and professional journeys. It stands as a modern-day parallel to the timeless lessons from the Ramayana, reaffirming the power of support in the battle against life's inner and outer demons.

## The Role of Mindfulness and Self-Reflection

### *Lesson from the Ramayana*

Amidst the epic battles and profound dilemmas, Lord Rama's moments of introspection and guidance from sagacious mentors stand out as crucial elements in his journey. These instances of mindfulness and self-reflection are pivotal, providing Rama with the clarity and tranquility necessary to face his external and internal battles. This chapter delves into the role of mindfulness and self-reflection as indispensable tools in the quest for inner peace and clarity, drawing inspiration from Rama's journey.

Rama, during his exile and the ensuing challenges, often sought counsel from wise sages like Vasistha and Vishwamitra. These interactions were not merely discussions but moments of profound introspection, where Rama engaged in deep contemplation and reflection. These practices helped him understand the intricate dynamics of dharma (duty) and karma (action) and enabled him to make decisions that aligned with his core values and principles.

Mindfulness, in the context of Rama's journey, goes beyond mere meditation. It involves a heightened awareness of his thoughts, emotions, and surroundings, allowing him to remain centered amidst turmoil. This mindfulness is coupled with a consistent practice of self-reflection, where Rama examines his motivations, fears, and aspirations. These practices act as a compass, guiding him through the complexities of life and leadership, ensuring that his actions are not just reactive but are grounded in thoughtful consideration.

In the modern world, where the pace of life and the barrage of stimuli can be overwhelming, the practices of mindfulness and self-reflection become even more relevant. Mindfulness, as a practice of being fully present and engaged with the here and now, enables individuals to navigate the chaos of everyday life with a sense of calm and focus. Similarly, self-reflection allows individuals to understand their inner workings better, recognize their strengths and weaknesses, and make conscious choices that resonate with their true selves.

The integration of these practices in everyday life can lead to enhanced decision-making, improved emotional regulation, and a deeper sense of fulfillment. By regularly engaging in mindfulness and self-reflection, individuals can cultivate a sense of inner peace and clarity, much like Rama. This inward journey equips them to better handle external challenges, stay aligned with their core values, and navigate life's complexities with grace and wisdom.

### *Modern Application*

In today's fast-paced and complex world, the practices of mindfulness and self-reflection are increasingly recognized as essential tools for effective leadership and personal growth. For modern leaders and professionals, these practices offer a means to navigate the constant stream of decisions, challenges, and interactions with clarity and purpose. Mindfulness helps in maintaining a calm and focused mind, essential for making thoughtful decisions, enhancing creativity, and managing stress. Self-reflection, on the other hand, aids in understanding one's motivations, biases, and impact on others, leading to more authentic and empathetic leadership.

Organizations and individuals can incorporate mindfulness through various practices such as meditation, mindful breathing, or even mindful walking, encouraging a culture where present-moment awareness is valued. Self-reflection can be integrated into daily routines through journaling, contemplative practices, or regular feedback sessions. These practices not only improve mental and emotional well-being but also enhance overall productivity and interpersonal dynamics within teams.

### Satya Nadella and Microsoft

Satya Nadella's tenure as the CEO of Microsoft offers a notable example of integrating mindfulness and self-reflection into leadership. Since taking the helm at Microsoft, Nadella has emphasized the importance of empathy and self-awareness, both in his personal approach and as a part of the company's culture. His leadership style is reflective of his belief in the power of empathy, derived from his mindfulness practices and introspective nature.

Nadella's approach to revamping Microsoft's culture involved encouraging employees to be more empathetic, not only towards each other but also towards their customers. This shift was partly attributed to his own practice of mindfulness, which he credits for helping him develop a deeper sense of empathy and understanding. He has also been open about the role of self-reflection in shaping his leadership style and decisions, particularly in how he navigates challenges and interacts with his team.

Under Nadella's leadership, Microsoft has seen a significant turnaround, marked by an inclusive work culture, innovative product development, and impressive market performance. His approach illustrates how mindfulness and self-reflection can transform not just individual leaders but entire organizations, fostering environments where innovation, collaboration, and well-being are prioritized.

Conquering inner demons, a central theme drawn from the final battle in the Ramayana, resonates deeply within the context of our personal and professional lives. The epic confrontation between Rama and Ravana extends far beyond a physical skirmish, symbolizing the internal struggle each individual faces against doubt, fear, and moral quandary. This timeless narrative from the Ramayana serves as a powerful metaphor for the journey of self-discovery and mastery.

The essence of this struggle, as exemplified by Rama, lies in the recognition and acknowledgment of one's inner conflicts. It's a battle that demands honesty, introspection, and the courage to confront the darker aspects of our psyche. Rama's journey teaches us the value of facing our fears and doubts head-on, embracing them as part of our growth process.

The story underscores the importance of adhering to one's ethical convictions and moral courage. Rama's unwavering commitment to dharma, despite personal struggles and external pressures, illustrates the strength that comes from a life guided by integrity and righteousness. His example encourages us to hold fast to our core values, even in the face of daunting challenges.

Equally vital is the role of a supportive network in our battles against inner demons. The solidarity and encouragement from allies, as seen in Rama's journey, emphasize the transformative power of having a strong support system. In times of internal turmoil, the guidance, understanding, and support from those around us can be the catalyst for overcoming our deepest fears and achieving personal triumph.

Finally, the practice of mindfulness and self-reflection, as mirrored in Rama's introspective moments, is a crucial tool for gaining clarity and peace. In our fast-paced, often tumultuous lives, these practices provide a sanctuary for self-awareness and contemplation, helping us align our actions with our deepest convictions.

The lessons from Rama's final battle transcend the boundaries of time and culture, offering timeless principles for personal growth and ethical living. They encourage us to embark on a journey of self-confrontation and mastery, leading us towards a life of purpose, integrity, and fulfillment. The Ramayana, in its rich and multifaceted narrative, thus remains a beacon of wisdom, guiding us in our quest to conquer our inner demons and achieve a harmonious balance in life.

# Chapter 11

# The Return to Ayodhya: Fulfillment and Legacy

As the golden chariot of Lord Rama, Sita, and Lakshman glides into the horizon, the ancient city of Ayodhya awakens in a kaleidoscope of emotions. The air, thick with the scent of blooming flowers and the melody of ringing temple bells, bears witness to a moment etched in eternity. The triumphant return of Rama and his companions to Ayodhya, marking the end of their arduous exile, is more than a mere historical event in the Ramayana; it is a crescendo of fulfillment and the dawn of an enduring legacy.

"Their path was lit by rejoicing stars, as though the heavens themselves wished to join in the celebration of Rama's return," writes Valmiki, capturing the ethereal essence of this moment. This return was not just a physical journey, but also a symbolic transition from trials and tribulations to the rightful realization of destiny. It is a testament to the unwavering commitment to dharma (righteous duty), resilience in the face of adversity, and the ultimate triumph of virtue.

The city of Ayodhya, depicted in the Ramayana as a realm of unparalleled splendor and prosperity, mirrors the collective joy and anticipation of its inhabitants. Their king, a paragon of virtue and an embodiment of divine will, returns to reclaim not just his throne but also the hearts of his people. The scenes of jubilation, the tears of joy, and the overwhelming sense of relief paint a vivid picture of a kingdom reunited with its beloved ruler.

As we delve into the layers of this historic homecoming, we find its relevance resonating through the corridors of time. The principles that guided Rama - truth, duty, honor, and compassion - are not confined to the realms of ancient epics. They are beacons that can illuminate the path of modern leadership and personal growth. This chapter aims to unravel these timeless lessons, offering insights into how fulfilling one's duties can lead to the creation of a legacy that transcends generations.

Accompanied by vivid sensory details, thoughtful quotes, and compelling storytelling, this exploration serves as an invitation to journey back to the heart of Ayodhya. It beckons us to transcend the boundaries of the text and venture into the depths of our own lives, posing a challenge to discover our paths to fulfillment and to forge legacies that resonate across time.

This narrative invites introspection and application, not just in the grand tales of yore but in the nuanced chapters of our personal journeys. It's an exploration of how ancient wisdom can guide modern lives, encouraging readers to align their actions with values that have stood the test of time. Through this journey, we'll uncover how the return to Ayodhya is not just a tale of triumph but a blueprint for living a life that balances duty, compassion, and personal growth.

## The Journey Back To Ayodhya

As the golden sun rises over Ayodhya, a wave of jubilation sweeps across the kingdom. The air, rich with the scent of blooming flowers and festive incense, carries the sound of tablas and sitars, creating a symphony of celebration. Today, Ayodhya's heart beats in unison, eagerly awaiting the return of Lord Rama, Sita, and Lakshman. This day marks not just the end of an arduous exile, but the dawn of a new era of fulfillment and legacy.

Rama's return to Ayodhya signifies more than the conclusion of his exile; it represents a profound transformation. The journey, filled with trials and tribulations, has carved deep lessons into the hearts of Rama, Sita, and Lakshman. Rama's wisdom, tempered by his trials, now bears a blend of strength and compassion. Sita, embodying grace under pressure, emerges as a figure of resilience and dignity. Lakshman, the embodiment of loyalty and courage, stands as an unwavering pillar of support.

Ayodhya, in anticipation of their return, is a canvas of joy and hope. Every street corner, every home, is adorned with vibrant decorations, and the air resonates with music and laughter. The city, pulsating with energy, reflects the collective spirit of its people, ready to welcome back their beloved prince and his companions.

The path back to Ayodhya is not just a physical journey but a spiritual odyssey. Rama, Sita, and Lakshman traverse through a landscape of self-discovery, each step bringing them closer to understanding the intricate balance of duty, love, and righteousness. This journey back is a testament to their growth, a journey where each challenge faced and each obstacle overcome has been a stepping stone to their inner evolution.

In Ayodhya, the air is thick with anticipation. The city, decked in its finest, is a spectacle of joyous fervor. The people, from the elders to the children, are united in their excitement. Stories of Rama's valor and Sita's grace are shared, creating a constellation of admiration and inspiration. The city, once shadowed by Rama's absence, now sparkles, ready to embrace its heroes.

## Ayodhya's Jubilant Welcome

As the first rays of dawn kissed the spires of Ayodhya, a palpable excitement stirred the air. The streets, adorned with marigold garlands and silk banners, wore the hues of a resplendent sunrise. The sound of conch shells and the rhythmic beat of dholaks echoed through the air, announcing the long-awaited return of Lord Rama, Sita, and Lakshman.

The entire city was a spectacle of joy and grandeur. Homes and marketplaces alike were festooned with colorful lights, and the fragrance of incense filled the air, mingling with the aromas of sumptuous feasts being prepared. As described in the Ramayana, "The city was decorated like a bride, radiating happiness and prosperity." The people of Ayodhya, young and old, danced in the streets, their faces beaming with joy. It was as if the city itself had come alive, pulsating with energy and happiness.

The royal palace was a scene of emotional reunion. King Dasharatha's spirit, though departed, seemed to smile down upon the joyful return of his son. Queen Kausalya's eyes, often filled with tears of longing, now sparkled with unshed tears of joy. The reunion of Rama with his brothers, particularly the heartfelt embrace with Bharata, was a moment that transcended the bounds of time, etching itself into the hearts of all who witnessed it.

Ayodhya's celebration was not just a display of joy but also a chorus of cultural and traditional richness. The city resonated with the melodies of classical ragas, each note capturing the essence of the moment. The streets were lined with performers enacting scenes from Rama's life, a tradition that kept the epic alive in the hearts of the people. Women dressed in vibrant saris performed folk dances, their movements narrating the story of Rama's victory.

This historic moment in Ayodhya offers more than a tale of triumph; it provides insights into the power of unity, resilience, and the human spirit. It teaches us that no challenge is insurmountable when faced with unwavering determination and hope. The celebration in Ayodhya serves as a reminder to cherish our victories, both big and small, and to find joy in the collective happiness of our communities.

While the grandeur of Ayodhya's celebration paints a picture of perfection, it also invites us to ponder upon the emotions of those who awaited Rama's return. It challenges us to empathize with the struggles behind the smiles, the resilience in the face of adversity, and the strength of spirit that kept Ayodhya's hope alive.

As a reader, imagine being a part of this grand celebration. What role would you play? Would you be a musician, a dancer, a storyteller, or simply a joyful participant? Reflect on how you celebrate your personal victories and those of your community. How can you bring the spirit of Ayodhya's celebration into your life and the lives of those around you?

## Reuniting with Bharata: A Lesson in Forgiveness and Brotherhood

As Lord Rama steps over the threshold of Ayodhya, the air is thick with anticipation, not just of a king's return but of a reunion steeped in profound emotional depths. The anticipation of meeting Bharata, who had humbly renounced the throne during Rama's absence, creates a palpable sense of expectancy. Their reunion is a mosaic of complex emotions, culminating in a deeply moving moment of forgiveness and mutual respect.

The Ramayana eloquently captures this moment: "As Rama and Bharata locked in an embrace, the years of longing and separation dissolved into the ether, forging an unbreakable bond of brotherhood, stronger and more profound than ever." This emotive description brings to life the sensory experience of their reunion - the warmth of their embrace, the mingling of joy and tears, and the collective sigh of relief and happiness that swept through the onlookers.

Bharata's selfless act of governing Ayodhya in Rama's stead, prioritizing duty and brotherly love over personal ambition, stands as a towering example of loyalty and integrity. His respect for Rama's right to the throne transcends the mere relinquishing of power; it is an act of profound moral conviction. In contrast, Rama's acceptance of Bharata is not mere forgiveness; it is an acknowledgment of Bharata's profound devotion and sacrifice. Their reunion is a celebration of their individual virtues and the strength of their brotherly bond.

This narrative is not just a tale from a bygone era but a lesson in the true essence of forgiveness and understanding. It challenges the reader to reflect on their perceptions of forgiveness. Is it merely about letting go of grudges, or is it more about empathizing with others' situations and intentions?

In the spirit of Rama and Bharata's reunion, let us embark on a journey of introspection and shared learning. As you delve into this chapter, I invite you to pause and reflect on your own experiences. Think back to a moment in your life when you faced a misunderstanding or conflict with someone close to you. How did you navigate through this challenge? Did your resolution bring about a newfound strength in your relationship, akin to the rekindled bond between Rama and Bharata?

I encourage you to jot down your thoughts and feelings about this experience. What emotions surfaced during this period? Was there a moment of realization or empathy that guided you towards resolution? How did this experience reshape your understanding of forgiveness and brotherhood?

As you write, consider how your story parallels the emotional depth and the journey of reconciliation seen in Rama and Bharata's reunion. Reflect on the lessons you learned and how they have influenced your relationships since.

Furthermore, if you feel comfortable, I urge you to share your story with others. Whether it's through a discussion forum, a small group, or even with a friend, sharing these personal narratives can be a powerful way to foster empathy and understanding. It helps create a community where experiences are not just shared but also serve as catalysts for growth and deeper connection.

Through this exercise, you're not only engaging with the timeless wisdom of the Ramayana but also weaving its teachings into the fabric of your life. By embracing the essence of brotherhood and the power of forgiveness, just as Rama and Bharata did, you're contributing to a world that values empathy, understanding, and the strength of human connections.

## Reintegrating Sita: Overcoming Societal Challenges with Faith and Resilience

The return of Sita to Ayodhya was a moment of emotional complexity. The streets, alive with the fanfare of Rama's return, carried an undercurrent of whispers and veiled glances directed towards Sita. Despite her unwavering loyalty, she faced the trials of public doubt and skepticism. The Ramayana captures this duality with poignant clarity, reflecting the juxtaposition of joyous celebration and underlying suspicion.

In the face of societal judgment, Sita's resilience and grace emerge as lessons of inner strength and self-respect. Her poised demeanor in dealing with public scrutiny illustrates an extraordinary level of fortitude and dignity. Sita's experience is a narrative of standing firm in one's truth, despite external doubts. It is a testament to maintaining integrity and grace under pressure, offering profound insights into the strength of character.

Rama's belief in Sita's fidelity, despite the societal murmurs, highlights the importance of trust and conviction in leadership. His unwavering support for Sita, in the face of public opinion, underscores a leader's duty to uphold truth and righteousness. This aspect of the Ramayana delves into the challenges leaders face in balancing personal convictions with societal expectations, emphasizing the necessity of moral courage in governance.

This part of the Ramayana serves as a mirror to our contemporary society, where judgments and perceptions often cloud reality. It invites readers to question how often they let societal opinions influence their beliefs and actions. This segment of the narrative encourages a deeper understanding of integrity and the courage to stand by one's convictions, even when they go against the tide of public opinion.

As you delve into the story of Sita's return to Ayodhya and navigate the complexities of her situation, it's an opportunity to turn the lens inwards and reflect on your own life. Think about a time when you faced societal judgment or had to stand up for your beliefs. How did you respond? Did you feel the weight of external opinions, and how did you manage to stay true to your convictions?

Consider journaling about this experience. Detail the emotions you felt, the challenges you faced, and how you overcame them. Were there moments when you doubted yourself? How did you find the strength to maintain your integrity? This exercise is not just about recounting an experience; it's about understanding the depth of your resilience and the power of your convictions.

If you're comfortable, share your story in a discussion group or with a trusted friend. Engaging in conversation about these experiences can be incredibly insightful. It allows for a deeper understanding of how we, much like Sita, navigate the complex interplay of personal integrity and societal expectations. Through sharing and listening, we often find common ground, learning that our struggles with judgment and conviction are universal experiences, each with unique nuances.

This reflection is your journey of connecting an ancient narrative to your personal story. It serves as a reminder of the timeless nature of these challenges and the enduring strength of the human spirit to overcome them.

## Rama's Coronation and Governance

The coronation of Lord Rama as the king of Ayodhya marks a pivotal moment in the Ramayana, symbolizing not just the return of a rightful ruler but the dawn of a new era of governance and moral rectitude.

The day of Rama's coronation was imbued with a sense of grandeur and sanctity. The air was filled with the scent of sandalwood and jasmine, as priests chanted Vedic hymns. The citizens of Ayodhya gathered in multitudes, their eyes reflecting the pride and joy of witnessing their beloved prince ascend the throne. As described in the ancient texts, "The coronation of Rama was like the rising of the sun, bringing light and life to the world." The ceremony was a blend of solemn rituals and joyous celebrations, reflecting the profound significance of this event.

Rama's approach to governance was characterized by his unwavering commitment to dharma (righteous duty) and justice. He was a ruler who listened to his subjects, respected the wise counsel of his advisors, and made decisions that reflected the welfare of all. His leadership style was not about asserting power but about serving his people with humility and integrity. This approach to governance, grounded in ethical and moral principles, set a high standard for leaders of all times.

The concept of Ram Rajya (the reign of Rama) has been heralded as the epitome of an ideal rule. It was a time when truth, duty, and justice were the pillars of governance. The Ramayana states, "Under Rama's rule, the people were happy, the land was fertile, and there was neither fear nor want." Ram Rajya symbolizes an era where the ruler's primary duty was the happiness and prosperity of the people, transcending personal agendas or biases.

Rama's governance offers profound insights into contemporary leadership and management principles. His style of inclusive and ethical leadership, his emphasis on justice and equality, and his commitment to the welfare of his subjects serve as guiding principles for modern leaders. In a world where leadership is often challenged by ethical dilemmas and complex socio-political dynamics, Rama's approach provides a blueprint for compassionate, fair, and effective governance.

Rama's governance challenges to question and reassess the conventional notions of power and leadership. It invites a reevaluation of what constitutes true leadership – is it authority and control, or is it service and integrity? By reflecting on Rama's leadership style, you are encouraged to explore new dimensions of ethical leadership and its application in various aspects of modern life.

To bring these lessons closer to everyday experience, you are encouraged to engage in activities that mirror Rama's leadership principles. For instance, involve making a decision at work or in personal life based on ethical considerations rather than convenience or self-interest, thereby practicing Rama's principles of leadership.

## Lessons in Fulfillment and Legacy

Lord Rama's return to Ayodhya marks not just a triumphant end to his challenging exile, but the dawning of an epoch replete with profound personal fulfillment and the establishment of an enduring legacy. This momentous homecoming, vividly captured in the Ramayana, transcends the physical journey, symbolizing a spiritual crescendo that Rama reaches after years of trials and tribulations. The streets of Ayodhya come alive in a cascade of colors, sounds, and emotions, illustrating a vivid echo of sensory richness. The air vibrates with jubilation, the colors of festivities paint the city in hues of joy and the people's exuberant cheers resonate with deep-seated relief and happiness. This moment is not just a celebration of Rama's return but a collective sigh of fulfillment, marking the end of an arduous chapter and the beginning of a golden era.

Rama's enduring legacy, intricately woven through the Ramayana's narrative, transcends his role as a monarch and elevates him to a timeless epitome of ethical leadership and moral fortitude. His reign, often idealized as 'Ram Rajya', is not just a historical or mythical reference; it's a concept that has permeated through centuries as the benchmark for just, compassionate, and righteous governance. In this golden era, prosperity, justice, and harmony are not mere aspirations but tangible realities, creating an enduring paradigm of leadership that transcends the boundaries of time and geography.

In the modern context, Rama's story is not just a reflection of past ideals but a beacon for contemporary leadership. His unwavering dedication to duty, even in the face of daunting personal sacrifices, stands as a testament to the power of ethical governance and principled leadership. This narrative challenges today's leaders to introspect deeply about the legacies they wish to forge. It raises pivotal questions about the essence of true leadership: How does one navigate the intricate balance between personal ambition and ethical responsibility? What does it mean to lead with a steadfast commitment to integrity, justice, and righteousness?

## Carrying the Legacy Forward

In the intricate weave of contemporary leadership, the timeless principles of Rama's reign in Ayodhya, characterized by fairness, justice, and compassion, stand as beacons of inspiration. Drawing from the ancient wisdom of the Ramayana, this chapter delves into the practical application of these principles in today's leadership scenarios, offering a roadmap for modern leaders to navigate their roles with integrity and benevolence.

## Visionary Leadership: The Essence of Rama's Reign

Rama's rule, often eulogized as 'Ram Rajya', epitomized a kingdom where fairness and justice were not mere ideals but tangible realities. His leadership style, marked by a deep empathy for his subjects and an unwavering commitment to righteousness, serves as a blueprint for modern leaders. In a world often marred by inequality and injustice, Rama's example urges leaders to adopt a vision that transcends the pursuit of power or profit, to one that upholds the welfare of all stakeholders.

## Fairness in Decision Making: A Modern Imperative

The concept of fairness in governance, as demonstrated by Rama, can be a guiding principle for leaders today. In business or politics, decisions made with a fair and just lens can foster trust and loyalty among team members and constituents. A quote from the Ramayana eloquently captures this sentiment, "Justice, like a beacon, shines brightest in the darkest of times." Integrating fairness into every decision ensures that the benefits of leadership are equitably distributed, creating a harmonious and productive environment.

## Compassionate Leadership: Beyond the Boardroom

Rama's compassion extended beyond mere rule; it was a reflection of his profound understanding of human emotions and needs. Today's leaders can emulate this by cultivating a leadership style that prioritizes empathy and understanding. This could mean creating inclusive workplaces, fostering a culture of open communication, or implementing policies that consider the diverse needs of their teams. Compassion, as Rama showed, is a powerful tool that can transform workplaces, communities, and societies.

## Infusing Ancient Wisdom into Modern Practice

Imagine you're at a crossroads in your professional or personal life, facing a decision that impacts not just you but those around you. How do you choose the path of fairness and compassion, as exemplified by Rama? This segment of the chapter invites you, the reader, to actively engage with the principles of Rama's governance through interactive exercises and thought-provoking challenges.

## Challenge 1: The Fairness Exercise

Think of a recent conflict or decision-making scenario at your workplace. Put yourself in the shoes of Rama: How would you have navigated this situation to ensure fairness and justice for all parties involved? Reflect on the outcome and consider writing down the steps you would take. This exercise aims to cultivate your decision-making skills, emphasizing fairness as a core value.

## Challenge 2: Compassionate Leadership Project

Initiate a project in your community or workplace that reflects the essence of compassionate governance. This could range from organizing a community welfare program to creating a more inclusive team environment at work. Document your journey: the challenges you face, the solutions you implement, and the impact of your actions. Share your story with others to inspire and spread the values of empathetic leadership.

## Reflection and Discussion

After completing these challenges, take a moment to reflect on your experiences. How did these exercises change your perspective on leadership? Engage in discussions with peers or mentors about your insights and learnings. This dialogue can be a powerful tool for deepening your understanding and application of Rama's principles in modern contexts.

## The Living Legacy

By participating in these interactive challenges, you're not just learning about Rama's leadership; you're embodying it. Each decision you make, influenced by fairness and compassion, contributes to a living legacy of ethical leadership. This section of the chapter is not just about reading and understanding—it's about action and transformation. Embrace these principles in your daily life and become a torchbearer of Rama's timeless wisdom in the modern world.

## Embracing Timeless Wisdom for Future Generations

As the narrative of Lord Rama's return to Ayodhya unfolds, it transcends the boundaries of time and geography, resonating deeply with the human spirit. The Ramayana, in its poetic grandeur, captures the essence of this moment, "As Rama stepped into Ayodhya, the city blossomed anew, mirroring the renewal within his own heart." This imagery serves not just as a conclusion to an epic journey but as a beacon of hope and wisdom for generations to come.

## The Enduring Impact of Rama's Return

The story of Rama's return is more than a tale of triumph; it is a saga of resilience, faith, and the unwavering pursuit of dharma. The joyous celebration in Ayodhya, with streets alive with music and hearts brimming with joy, is a powerful symbol of the human yearning for justice, harmony, and moral integrity. This narrative invites us to reflect on our own journey towards ethical and compassionate living.

## Applying Ancient Wisdom in Contemporary Life

In a world that often prizes material success over moral values, Rama's story offers a counter-narrative. It encourages us to find fulfillment in upholding ethical principles and contributing to the greater good. Imagine applying Rama's principles in unexpected realms of life—perhaps in making eco-conscious choices that benefit the planet, or in choosing honesty over deceit in challenging business scenarios. Such choices embody Rama's legacy in everyday actions.

## Challenging Stereotypes

Rama's return challenges us to rethink our perceptions of success and leadership. Instead of viewing power through the lens of conquest or material gain, we are inspired to see leadership as a responsibility towards righteousness and welfare. Engage in discussions that question and expand these conventional beliefs, creating a ripple effect of change.

## Engage and Transform

To truly embody the lessons from Ayodhya, embark on an interactive journey. Challenge yourself to a week of making choices aligned with dharma, journal your experiences, and share your reflections with others. Organize community discussions or workshops centered around the themes of the Ramayana, exploring its relevance in modern times.

As we reach the conclusion of this exploration into Rama's triumphant return to Ayodhya, it's essential to reflect on the enduring legacy of this momentous event. The Ramayana tells us, "Rama's return was not just the end of an exile, but the beginning of an era." This statement captures the essence of Rama's journey – a journey that resonates across time, impacting generation after generation with its profound lessons.

The celebration that enveloped Ayodhya upon Rama's return was more than just a festivity; it was a collective sigh of relief, a culmination of hope, and a celebration of virtue and righteousness. The city, once clouded in despair during Rama's absence, was now alight with joy, the streets echoing with songs of welcome, the air fragrant with the scent of flowers. This vibrant scene is a powerful reminder of the joy that follows the fulfillment of duty and the restoration of dharma.

Rama's return and subsequent reign, termed 'Ram Rajya', symbolize an ideal state of governance, where fairness, justice, and compassion prevail. This ideal continues to resonate in the modern context, challenging leaders and individuals alike to emulate these principles in their lives and work. Rama's commitment to his duties, despite personal sacrifices, serves as an inspiration, urging us to consider the impact of our actions on the greater good.

The story of Rama is not just a tale of ancient times but a narrative that holds significant lessons for contemporary society. It prompts us to question our understanding of leadership, governance, and ethical conduct. How do we balance personal desires with societal responsibilities? In what ways can we integrate the principles of 'Ram Rajya' into our leadership styles, workplaces, and communities? These are questions that push us to think beyond the conventional, to re-examine our values and the legacy we wish to leave behind.

Let us carry forward the timeless wisdom of Rama's return to Ayodhya, applying its lessons to our lives. Whether in leading a team, making decisions that affect others, or standing up for what is right, we have the opportunity to reflect the virtues exemplified by Rama. In doing so, we contribute to a legacy that transcends time, inspiring future generations to uphold values of righteousness, compassion, and integrity.

# Chapter 12

# Integrating the Ramayana's Wisdom into Modern Life

The Ramayana, an ancient epic revered across centuries, stands not merely as a tale of heroism and morality but as a profound guidebook brimming with timeless wisdom. This narrative, deeply rooted in the cultural and spiritual soil of human history, extends far beyond its mythological characters and fantastical elements, offering insights that resonate with the core of human existence.

At the heart of the Ramayana is the concept of 'Dharma' or righteousness, exemplified by Lord Rama. Despite facing heart-wrenching trials and tribulations, Rama's unwavering adherence to his dharma illuminates the path of ethical living. It is through Rama's choices, often marked by personal sacrifice, that the epic communicates the profound message that true strength lies in living a life aligned with one's moral and ethical values.

Characters like Sita, embodying the epitome of sacrifice and devotion, and Lakshmana, the paradigm of unwavering loyalty, add layers of depth to the narrative. Sita's endurance in the face of adversity and Lakshmana's relentless support for Rama are powerful reminders of the strength inherent in selflessness. Their stories weave a symphony of devoted love and loyalty that transcends the tests of time.

The Ramayana is a saga of overcoming adversity through resilience, intelligence, and fortitude. Whether it is Rama's journey through exile, Sita's abduction, or the monumental battle against Ravana, each episode is a testament to facing life's hurdles with courage and wisdom. These narratives impart the lesson that life's battles, both external and internal, are surmountable with the right blend of valor, intellect, and perseverance.

The alliance between Rama and Hanuman, and the solidarity of the Vanara army, underscore the power of friendship and unity. The epic beautifully demonstrates that collective strength and harmonious collaboration can lead to extraordinary achievements, surpassing even the most formidable challenges.

The Ramayana delves deeply into the human condition, exploring a spectrum of emotions and relationships. It addresses the complexities of duty, desire, jealousy, and redemption, providing a rich understanding of the diverse facets of human nature and relationships.

The timeless teachings of the Ramayana hold profound relevance in today's world. In our personal journeys, the principles of dharma can guide ethical decision-making and moral integrity. In leadership and governance, Rama's example inspires fairness, compassion, and righteousness. In the realm of personal relationships, the bonds between Rama, Sita, Lakshmana, and Hanuman offer insights into loyalty, trust, and unconditional support.

The Ramayana, thus, is not just an epic to be revered; it is a living, breathing guide that echoes through generations, offering wisdom and insights applicable to the myriad dimensions of life. Its teachings, when contemplated and integrated into our daily lives, have the potential to enlighten, transform, and elevate the human spirit.

## The Relevance of Ramayana in Contemporary Society

In the ever-evolving landscape of our contemporary world, the ancient epic of the Ramayana emerges not as a relic of the past but as a beacon of wisdom, casting light on modern-day challenges. This lesson delves into the profound parallels between the timeless themes of the Ramayana and the intricacies of our current societal and personal struggles.

The Ramayana, a narrative steeped in moral complexities and heroic endeavors, mirrors the dilemmas we face today. Lord Rama's embodiment of righteousness and his journey resonate in a world grappling with ethical quandaries and moral ambiguity. His choices, often marred by sacrifice and struggle, offer a guiding star for navigating the gray areas of modern ethics and responsibilities. The Ramayana states, "In a world torn by conflicts and differences, Rama stands as a symbol of reconciliation." This ancient wisdom encourages us to seek harmony amidst discord, a lesson ever so pertinent in our divisive times.

In the realm of leadership and governance, the Ramayana presents a blueprint for just and compassionate rule. Rama's approach to kingship, where the welfare of his subjects was paramount, provides insights into servant leadership. His reign, known as Ram Rajya, is remembered as a period of fairness, prosperity, and justice. This ideal can inspire modern leaders to prioritize the well-being of their people and lead with integrity. The epic questions, "What is the duty of a ruler if not to serve and protect his people?" urging today's leaders to reflect on their roles as custodians of their community's trust and welfare.

The intricate relationships in the Ramayana, whether it's the deep bond between Rama and Sita, the unwavering loyalty of Lakshmana, or the devoted friendship with Hanuman, provide profound insights into our interpersonal dynamics. These relationships highlight the values of trust, commitment, and sacrifice, which are as crucial in nurturing personal relationships today as they were in the epic. In an age where relationships can be complex and challenging, the Ramayana's narratives offer a lens to view and understand the nuances of human connections.

Sita's resilience in the face of adversity and her unyielding spirit provide a powerful example for overcoming personal struggles. Her journey speaks to the strength required to face societal judgments and personal trials, resonating with individuals battling against odds in their lives. The Ramayana gently reminds us, "The strength of the spirit can conquer the trials of the flesh," encouraging us to find fortitude within.

The principles of the Ramayana find their relevance in various aspects of contemporary life. In the corporate world, the ideals of ethical leadership, teamwork, and integrity can be derived from the epic. In personal growth, the themes of resilience, moral strength, and self-reflection are pertinent. In societal dynamics, the lessons of compassion, justice, and unity offer a pathway to a more harmonious coexistence.

Thus, the Ramayana, far from being an ancient tale, is a living narrative that continues to provide guidance, inspiration, and solace. Its stories and characters, though set in a distant past, reflect the universal human experience, making it a timeless companion in our journey through life.

## Personal Growth and Self-Improvement: Lessons from the Ramayana

In the intricate narrative of the Ramayana, each character and their journey provide profound insights for personal growth and self-improvement. By embodying the virtues of Rama, Sita, Hanuman, and others, we can navigate the complexities of modern life with a blend of wisdom, strength, and compassion.

Rama's life is a testament to living with righteousness and integrity. In every action and decision, he exemplifies unwavering adherence to dharma (duty), even in the face of personal loss. His journey encourages us to make choices that are aligned with our values and principles. The Ramayana eloquently states, "In the heart of Rama, dharma was his compass." In our daily lives, this translates to making ethical decisions, being honest in our interactions, and upholding our moral values, even when it's challenging.

Sita's strength and grace in the face of adversity are remarkable. Her unwavering dignity during her abduction and subsequent trials teach us the power of resilience. Her journey is a reminder that our circumstances do not define us; our reactions and inner strength do. Sita's story urges us to face life's challenges with grace and to maintain our integrity even in the darkest of times.

Hanuman's devotion and service to Rama are unparalleled. His journey is filled with lessons on the power of devotion, the importance of selfless service, and the strength of faith. Hanuman teaches us that with faith, determination, and dedication, no challenge is too great. His famous leap to Lanka, driven by sheer devotion and resolve, serves as a metaphor for overcoming personal obstacles with faith and perseverance.

Incorporating these virtues into our daily life can be transformative. When faced with a moral dilemma, asking oneself, "What would Rama do?" can provide clarity. Emulating Sita's resilience can help us navigate our personal struggles with dignity. Drawing inspiration from Hanuman's devotion can motivate us to serve others selflessly and pursue our goals with unwavering focus.

The Ramayana also challenges us to question stereotypes and societal norms. For example, analyzing Rama's decision-making process encourages critical thinking about leadership and responsibility. Reflecting on Sita's trials prompts discussions on societal judgments and personal strength.

To bring these lessons to life, readers can engage in activities like journaling their thoughts on how they would handle similar situations faced by these characters or discussing with peers how these ancient lessons are relevant in modern contexts.

The Ramayana offers a treasure trove of wisdom for personal growth and self-improvement. Its characters and their journeys provide timeless lessons that, when applied, can lead to a fulfilling and principled life.

## Ethical Leadership and Governance: Learning from Rama's Example

The Ramayana, through Lord Rama's reign, offers an unparalleled example of ethical leadership and governance. Rama's approach to ruling Ayodhya was marked by fairness, justice, and empathy, principles that can profoundly influence modern leadership and organizational practices.

Rama's rule, often referred to as 'Ram Rajya', was an era where the welfare of the people was paramount. The Ramayana describes this period as one where "Truth and virtue reigned, and the citizens lived in harmony and contentment." This ideal governance was not just a result of Rama's divine lineage but his commitment to ethical principles. He listened to his subjects' voices, ensuring that justice was accessible to all. His decisions, though sometimes arduous, were always in the interest of dharma (righteousness) and the greater good.

In today's organizational settings, Rama's style of leadership is more relevant than ever. Leaders can emulate his approach by prioritizing ethical decision-making and transparency. Fostering an environment where honesty and integrity are valued lays the foundation for a just and fair workplace.

For instance, when facing ethical dilemmas, leaders can ask, "What would be the most righteous course of action?" much like Rama would. This could mean making tough decisions that might not be the easiest or most profitable but are morally right and beneficial in the long term.

The story of Rama challenges many conventional notions of power and leadership. It encourages leaders to redefine success not just in terms of financial gains or personal accolades but as the ability to positively impact people's lives. This perspective can lead to more compassionate and inclusive leadership practices.

A modern-day parallel to Rama's ethical governance can be seen in the leadership approach of New Zealand Prime Minister Jacinda Ardern. Her handling of various crises, including the Christchurch mosque shootings and the COVID-19 pandemic, reflected an empathetic and morally sound approach. Her decisions, guided by the welfare of her citizens and a strong moral compass, garnered international praise and demonstrated how ethical leadership could lead to trust and respect from both subordinates and peers.

Lord Rama's example in the Ramayana offers timeless lessons in ethical leadership and governance. By integrating his principles of fairness, justice, and empathy, modern leaders can create an environment of trust, integrity, and welfare, thereby redefining the essence of successful leadership.

## Cultivating Strong Relationships and Community: Insights from the Ramayana

The Ramayana is not just an epic narrative of heroes and demons; it is a profound exploration of the intricacies of human relationships. The relationships in the Ramayana, whether it's the bond between Rama and his brothers, his love for Sita, or his camaraderie with Hanuman and the Vanaras, offer invaluable insights into building and maintaining strong personal and professional bonds.

One of the most significant aspects of the Ramayana is the deep bond of loyalty and affection between Rama and his brothers, particularly Lakshmana. Lakshmana's decision to accompany Rama into exile, foregoing the comforts of the palace, is a testament to unwavering loyalty and fraternal love. The Ramayana narrates this bond beautifully, stating, "Wherever Rama went, Lakshmana followed like a shadow, unwavering in his devotion." This relationship teaches us the value of steadfast loyalty and support in both personal and professional spheres.

The Ramayana also emphasizes the importance of trust and respect in relationships. Rama's trust in Sita, even in the face of societal skepticism, and his respect for her dignity and choices, form the cornerstone of their relationship. In a professional context, this translates to building relationships based on mutual trust and respect, recognizing and valuing each individual's contributions and choices.

The alliance between Rama and the Vanaras, especially Hanuman, highlights the power of shared values and goals in forming strong bonds. The Vanaras rallied around Rama's cause, driven by shared values of righteousness and justice. In modern settings, this can be mirrored in building communities or teams centered around common objectives and shared beliefs, fostering a sense of unity and purpose.

These timeless principles from the Ramayana can be applied in various facets of contemporary life. For instance, in a corporate setting, the loyalty and support exemplified by Lakshmana can inspire team members to collaborate effectively, supporting each other through challenges. Similarly, the mutual respect and trust between Rama and Sita can guide modern leaders in fostering inclusive and respectful workplaces.

The Ramayana challenges us to look beyond superficial connections, urging us to cultivate relationships rooted in deeper values like trust, respect, and shared goals. It encourages us to question the transient nature of modern relationships and to strive for bonds that are enduring and meaningful.

The Ramayana offers a treasure trove of wisdom on cultivating strong relationships and a sense of community. By embracing these ancient yet timeless principles, we can enrich our personal and professional lives, creating bonds that are both fulfilling and enduring.

## Overcoming Challenges and Adversity: Gleaning Strength from the Ramayana

The Ramayana is a saga filled with daunting challenges and adversities, yet it is the manner in which its characters face these hurdles that offers enduring lessons. The epic is a rich source of strategies for dealing with life's obstacles, providing insights into harnessing inner strength and resilience.

A pivotal lesson from the Ramayana is facing challenges with unwavering courage and determination. Lord Rama's entire journey is marked by formidable obstacles, yet his approach to each challenge is defined by his valor and steadfastness. As the Ramayana states, "In the face of adversity, Rama stood unwavering, his resolve as firm as the mighty mountains." This highlights the importance of embracing challenges head-on, rather than shying away from them. In modern life, this translates to confronting difficulties with a positive mindset, viewing them as opportunities for growth and learning.

The characters of the Ramayana, particularly Sita, embody remarkable resilience. Despite facing extreme hardships, Sita's strength never falters. Her journey through adversity is marked by an inner resilience that is both inspiring and instructive. Her story teaches us that the core of resilience lies within, and it is this inner strength that enables one to withstand and emerge stronger from life's trials. In contemporary times, this lesson is crucial in navigating personal and professional challenges, encouraging individuals to find strength within themselves.

Hanuman's journey in the Ramayana is a testament to resourcefulness and adaptability. His ingenious methods in overcoming obstacles, such as his leap across the ocean, demonstrate the power of creative problem-solving. In today's fast-paced world, being resourceful and adaptable in the face of adversity is a valuable skill. Hanuman's example inspires us to think innovatively and find effective solutions to our problems.

The principles of courage, resilience, and resourcefulness from the Ramayana can be effectively applied in various scenarios today.

From dealing with workplace challenges to personal hardships, these lessons encourage us to approach difficulties with a positive mindset, harness our inner strength, and think creatively for solutions.

The Ramayana encourages us to question the conventional ways of dealing with challenges. Instead of succumbing to adversity, it inspires us to explore new avenues of facing and overcoming it. This approach can transform the way we perceive and handle difficulties in our lives.

The Ramayana offers profound insights into overcoming challenges and adversity. By embracing its lessons of courage, resilience, and resourcefulness, we can navigate the complexities of modern life with strength and confidence.

## The Path to Inner Peace and Harmony: Gleaning Spiritual Insights from the Ramayana

The Ramayana, more than an epic narrative, is a profound spiritual guide that offers timeless wisdom for achieving inner peace and harmony. Its teachings, deeply rooted in virtue and righteousness, illuminate the path to a balanced and fulfilling life.

The journey of Lord Rama in the Ramayana is not just an external quest but also an internal exploration of peace and harmony. Despite the turmoil and trials he faces, Rama remains anchored in serenity and moral integrity. As the Ramayana eloquently puts it, "In the eye of the storm, Rama stood serene, a beacon of tranquility amidst chaos." This highlights the importance of maintaining inner calm and composure, regardless of external circumstances. It teaches us that true peace comes from within and is attainable through adherence to one's principles and values.

One of the core teachings of the Ramayana is adherence to Dharma. Rama's unwavering commitment to his duties, even in the face of personal loss, underscores the importance of living a life aligned with one's ethical and moral duties. This alignment is key to achieving harmony in life. The Ramayana's message is clear: when actions are in harmony with Dharma, inner peace follows naturally. In the modern context, this translates to living authentically and making choices that align with one's true self and moral compass.

The Ramayana also offers insights into cultivating balanced relationships. The interactions between Rama and his allies, such as Sita, Lakshman, and Hanuman, demonstrate mutual respect, understanding, and support. These relationships are marked by a harmonious balance of love, duty, and devotion, providing a blueprint for nurturing healthy personal and professional relationships.

The principles of inner peace and harmony from the Ramayana are profoundly relevant in contemporary life. Amidst the hustle and stress of modern living, these teachings guide us to find balance, stay true to our ethical beliefs, and nurture harmonious relationships. They encourage us to look inward for peace and to live a life that is in harmony with our deepest values and principles.

The Ramayana challenges the modern notion that peace and harmony are solely external achievements. It directs us to explore inner peace as a foundation for a balanced life. The epic invites us to introspect, asking us to reconsider our perspectives on harmony and how we pursue it in our daily lives.

The Ramayana's teachings on inner peace and harmony offer profound spiritual insights. By embracing these timeless principles, we can navigate the complexities of modern life with a sense of balance, serenity, and fulfillment.

## Interactive Activities and Reflections: Engaging with the Ramayana's Teachings

The Ramayana, a reservoir of timeless wisdom, offers more than just stories; it presents principles that can profoundly impact our lives. To truly assimilate these teachings, engaging in interactive activities and reflections can be immensely beneficial. These exercises are designed not only to deepen understanding but also to encourage active application of the Ramayana's wisdom in various aspects of modern life.

### 1. Personal Dharma Assessment

- Activity:   Reflect on your personal values and principles. How do they align with your actions and decisions? Are there areas in your life where you feel a disconnect between your beliefs and your actions?

- Application:   Just as Rama's adherence to Dharma guided his choices, use this exercise to realign your actions with your personal values, ensuring they resonate with your true self.

### 2. Overcoming Your Lanka

- Activity:   Identify a personal challenge or 'Lanka' you face. Write down the obstacles, your fears, and potential strategies to overcome this challenge.

- Reflection: Drawing inspiration from Rama's journey, consider the strengths and support systems you can leverage to overcome your obstacles.

### 3. The Sita Resilience Journal

- Activity:  Keep a journal for a week, documenting moments where you faced adversity or judgment. Reflect on how you responded to these challenges and what you learned from them.

- Application:  Like Sita's resilience in the face of trials, use this journal to understand and grow your inner strength and resilience.

### 4. Hanuman's Teamwork Challenge

- Group Activity:  Organize a teamwork challenge in your community or workplace. It could be a collaborative project, a problem-solving task, or a community service event.

- Learning:  Reflect on the dynamics of teamwork and leadership. How do different strengths contribute to the success of a group, much like the diverse abilities of the Vanaras?

### 5. Rama's Leadership Dialogue

- Activity:  Write or role-play a dialogue between you and a leader you admire (real or fictional). Discuss a leadership dilemma and explore how they would approach it.

- Reflection:  Use this dialogue to gain insights into ethical leadership and decision-making, inspired by Rama's leadership style.

### 6. The Ayodhya Peace Walk

- Activity:  Organize a 'peace walk' in your local area, focusing on mindfulness and community harmony.

- Experience:  As you walk, reflect on the sense of peace and harmony that Rama brought to Ayodhya. How can you cultivate these qualities in your community?

These activities are not mere exercises; they are gateways to experiencing and integrating the profound lessons of the Ramayana. By actively engaging in these reflections and challenges, readers can bring the epic's wisdom to life, enriching their personal growth and contributing to their communities. Each step taken in this journey of reflection and action brings us closer to understanding the depth and relevance of the Ramayana's teachings in our modern world.

# Sankalpa

As we reach the culmination of our journey through "The Ramayana Code," it is my hope that the narratives and insights shared within these pages have not only enlightened but also inspired a *sankalpa* within you. This ancient concept—a resolve to pursue truth, righteousness, and wisdom—mirrors the quests of Rama and his companions, whose paths are etched in the annals of time not just as tales of valor but as beacons guiding us towards our higher selves.

In embracing the principles of Dharma, in seeking to embody the virtues of dedication, courage, and compassion, we engage in a continuous cycle of learning and growth. The Ramayana, with its intricate web of stories, characters, and morals, serves not as a mere recounting of historical events but as a living, breathing guide for navigating the complexities of life with integrity and purpose.

As you close this book, may the *sankalpa* kindled by these timeless teachings illuminate your path forward, inspiring you to carve your legacy in the spirit of the epic's enduring wisdom. The journey does not end here; it evolves, inviting us to delve deeper into the vast ocean of life's mysteries with an unwavering resolve to uncover the truth, uphold justice, and live a life of profound meaning.

May the journey of Rama inspire your own, and may your *sankalpa* guide you to your Ayodhya, where fulfillment, peace, and righteousness reign supreme.

9 7 9 8 8 9 2 7 7 8 2 7 5